Teaching in 2 Languages

D1258703

To the memory of my bilingual and bicultural grandmother,
Florence Adelman,
who led a life filled with love for and service to others.
And for Andre and Glenna
My hope and my future.

—Sharon

In honor of Baba Gita, Deda Grisha, Bula, and Zhoock
my multilingual grandparents
whose languages, ייִדיש, *latviešu,* русский, *and English,*
trace their religious, ethnic, and immigrant histories.

—Tatyana

Teaching in 2 Languages

A Guide for K–12 Bilingual Educators

Sharon Adelman Reyes
Tatyana Kleyn

Foreword by Ofelia García

CORWIN
A SAGE Company

For information:

Corwin
A SAGE Company
2455 Teller Road
Thousand Oaks, California 91320
(800) 233-9936
Fax: (800) 417-2466
www.corwin.com

SAGE Ltd.
1 Oliver's Yard
55 City Road
London EC1Y 1SP
United Kingdom

SAGE India Pvt. Ltd.
B 1/I 1 Mohan Cooperative
   Industrial Area
Mathura Road, New Delhi 110 044
India

SAGE Asia-Pacific Pte. Ltd.
33 Pekin Street #02-01
Far East Square
Singapore 048763

Printed in the United States of America

Library of Congress Cataloging-in-Publication Data

Reyes, Sharon Adelman.
Teaching in two languages: a guide for K–12 bilingual educators / Sharon Adelman Reyes and Tatyana Kleyn.
    p. cm.
Includes bibliographical references and index.
ISBN 978-1-4129-7802-6 (pbk.)

   1. Education, Bilingual—Study and teaching (Elementary) 2. Education, Bilingual—Study and teaching (Secondary) 3. Second language acquisition—Study and teaching (Elementary) 4. Second language acquisition—Study and teaching (Secondary) 5. Bilingualism in children. I. Kleyn, Tatyana. II. Title.

LC3275.R49 2010
370.117′5—dc22   2009038917

This book is printed on acid-free paper.

10   11   12   13   14   10 9 8 7 6 5 4 3 2 1

Acquisitions Editor:	Dan Alpert
Associate Editor:	Megan Bedell
Production Editor:	Cassandra Margaret Seibel
Typesetter:	C&M Digitals (P) Ltd.
Cover Designer:	Scott Van Atta

Contents

Foreword

Ofelia García

More bilingual students than ever are crowding the nation's schools, and yet, fewer bilingual teachers are being prepared to teach them. One of the greatest challenges in U.S. education today is the teaching of *emergent bilinguals*—students who speak another language at home and are also learning English and, in so doing, are becoming bilingual.

With the number of emergent bilingual students rising and accountability measures taking center stage in American education, it has become clear that specialized understandings are needed in order to ensure emergent bilinguals' English development, as well as their academic success. But a myopic view that sees these students *only* as limited English proficient (LEPs) or English language learners (ELLs) is shutting down visions of how to build on bilingual theoretical frameworks and use new bilingual strategies in order to meaningfully educate them.

Many institutions of higher education have developed new teacher education programs in an effort to meet the mounting needs of this emergent bilingual school population. But with the narrow focus on the teaching of English to ELLs and LEPs, many institutions have opted for Teaching English to Speakers of Other Languages (TESOL) programs that have shed all associations with bilingualism. At the same time, many programs to prepare bilingual teachers have shut down. The thinking is that the focus of teacher education has to be on English only, and that traditional bilingual education programs are outdated in an era of globalization and when classroom linguistic heterogeneity is rampant. But if we appropriate a more generous and broad focus for educating emergent bilinguals, rather than a narrow one of just teaching them English, it is obvious that bilingualism and bilingual strategies have to be part of the understandings of ALL teachers in the twenty-first century, including those who think of themselves as teaching in English only. In successfully teaching learners of English, all teachers develop the students' bilingualism.

That the teaching of English is frequently the only focus of education programs for emergent bilinguals is also evident in the publication of books for teachers. In the last decade, many good books on the topic of teaching ELLs have been published. As far as I'm aware, however, none has specifically focused on the use of bilingual strategies in classrooms. And not one book has been written specifically for bilingual teachers. Thus, this book by Reyes and Kleyn is in a league of its own, adopting a broader stance of what it means to educate emergent bilinguals for the twenty-first century.

That understanding is also reflected in the book's attention to content area instruction. Emergent bilinguals need to be educated meaningfully, and chapters on teaching mathematics, science, and social studies are included.

Although bilingual educators have been good advocates for children and have advanced important theoretical frameworks, the bilingual education field has suffered from unsystematic curricular innovations and few important pedagogical advances. We have paid attention to English language acquisition and English literacy pedagogy, but bilingual acquisition remains undertheorized, and pedagogies and strategies for the development of the additional language, and especially for the interaction of the two languages, have been poorly elaborated. Bilingual pedagogical practices that build on what I have called the *translanguaging* of bilingual communities (García, 2009) have also received little scholarly attention. Again, in this respect, Reyes and Kleyn make a unique contribution to teacher education, as well as to bilingual education scholarship. They focus on bilingual methodology and strategies that have received little attention in the past.

What makes this book so interesting for educators is the authors' ability to direct teachers and to awaken their imagination and nudge them to try new things. And yet, the book allows teachers freedom to choose and select different options that best serve their children, their classrooms, and their communities. At the core of each chapter are the sections titled Try This! These are a cry to break out of the mold, to take risks, to be bold and brave, to think beyond what is given, and to go beyond conventional wisdom and understanding. Reyes and Kleyn's years of experience as teachers and teacher educators, as well as their rich imagination and clear writing style, enable them to offer different options, to imagine different scenarios, and to show the different roads that may be taken. The teacher is empowered, but not coerced.

Another reason teachers will want to "Try This!" is precisely that they are the true protagonists of the book. This is a teachers' book—from teachers, for teachers, about teachers, with teachers. Reyes and Kleyn not only blend their own teaching expertise around the education of emergent bilinguals, but also incorporate the practices and voices of other teachers. Thus, while based in theoretical scholarly literature, the book starts and ends with the teachers' experience as the grounding force. The teachers' practice is not subservient to scholarship; instead, the theory flows from the teachers' experience.

In fact, it is the teacher who is the expert in this book. Reyes and Kleyn have chosen well the nine essential questions that frame and begin Chapters 1–9. But they shy away from becoming the authority who answers these questions according to their own ideologies and experience. Instead, the authors end each chapter with a teacher's response to the essential question. It is the work of the teacher that is honored, respected, and made essential in this book. The last word is that of the teacher.

The bilingual teacher this book supports is not the educator of the past, but the educator of the future. He or she is not necessarily a Spanish/English teacher, but may speak Hebrew, French, Russian, Chinese, Haitian Creole, Turkish, or another language. This teacher works not only in public schools, but also in private religious or secular schools, charter schools, or after-school programs. He or she is not concerned with the maintenance of a language other than English as in the past, or with a "heritage" language,[1] but with the development of the students' bilingualism for a future when bilingual discursive practices and translanguaging will be at the center of all interactions in the United States, as well as in the world.

Sometimes this teacher works in a bilingual classroom in a bilingual education program, teaching in both languages or in one or the other language, while thinking of the bilingual development of the students and of the interdependence of all their language practices. At other times he or she is working in an English-only program with a multilingual student body, and wants to know what can be done to build on the students' home language and bilingual practices. He or she mostly serves language minority students, but sometimes language majority students are also in the mix. For all students, the teacher's bilingual strategies are most important, as cross-cultural and multilingual understandings are constructed for a better future not only for the children, but also for our country. This teacher, with bilingual understandings and a commitment to deepen his or her knowledge and expertise, is the protagonist in this book.

I have felt honored to be asked to write the foreword for this book, for one because it is a great book that will be of great help to bilingual teachers, but more important because it extends and reshapes the work that I, along with many colleagues, did in the bilingual education program at The City College of New York in the 1980s and 1990s, where Kleyn now teaches. Throughout the years I have learned much from the work of Sharon Adelman Reyes as well as that of Tatyana Kleyn, who was a doctoral student at Teachers College when I was there. The work of teacher and student blends and merges, in much the same way that the work of Reyes and Kleyn, as scholars and teacher educators, come together with that of the teachers in this book. It is the multigenerational, multifaceted, multicultural, and multilingual efforts of many that will eventually bring equity and expertise to bear on the education of emergent bilinguals in the United States. I am convinced that this book makes an important contribution toward that important endeavor.

Ofelia García
The Graduate Center, City University of New York
PhD Program in Urban Education

NOTE

1. I have argued against the use of the term "heritage language speaker" because of its focus on the past in García, Ofelia. 2005. Positioning heritage languages in the United States. *Modern Language Journal 89*(4), 601–605.

REFERENCE

García, O. (2009). *Bilingual education in the 21st century: A global perspective.* Malden, MA: Wiley/Blackwell.

Preface

*B*ilingual teacher. If these words describe you (or your professional aspiration), you probably already know that just one word, *bilingual,* makes a huge difference in how you teach, in how others perceive you, and in who you are. Many books are written for teachers and preservice teachers; fewer are written for their bilingual counterparts. Here, then, is a book written especially with you, the bilingual teacher, in mind. It addresses not only specific approaches, methodologies, and strategies for teaching in bilingual classrooms, but also the social context that makes you so different—and so essential.

Today, in the United States, only a small percentage of students who need a bilingual education actually receive one. Most English language learners (ELLs), also known as *emergent bilingual students* (García, Kleifgen, & Falchi, 2007)[1], are taught in ways that neither value nor incorporate their native language or cultural heritage. These are the children and youth from homes where Arabic, Armenian, Cantonese, French, Haitian Creole, Hindi, Hmong, Japanese, Khmer, Korean, Lao, Mandarin, Navajo, Polish, Portuguese, Punjabi, Russian, Serbo-Croatian, Spanish, Tagalog, Urdu, Vietnamese, and many other languages are spoken. And their numbers are growing rapidly.

As García (2005) notes, "School districts in all regions of the nation are confronting the challenge of educating bilingual students" (p. 6). Demographers project that, 35 years from now, white students will be a minority in our educational system because the population of students who are both culturally and linguistically diverse will have risen dramatically (García & Cuellar, 2006).

Yet our nation faces a severe shortage of teachers who are prepared to teach such students by making modifications to the English-language curriculum. Even fewer are able to teach using the native languages of their students. On the national level, only 2.5% of teachers who are working with ELLs are professionally prepared to teach them (Ruíz-de-Velasco, Fix, & Clewell, 2000).

Even when ELLs have teachers who speak their native language, such teachers may not have been adequately prepared to teach bilingually. Although they are able to communicate with their students, they may flounder as they try to give their students access to the academic curriculum. Furthermore, bilingual teachers may feel isolated among their peers (Arce, 2004). To complicate this situation, while many educational resources exist for teachers who seek guidance in English as a second language (ESL) curriculum and pedagogy, the same is less true of resources in the realm of bilingual education in general and native language instruction in particular.

This book seeks to provide information and strategies that can assist in K–12 bilingual educational contexts. It can also be used as a much-needed resource for future bilingual teachers, as well as for current teachers placed in bilingual classrooms without adequate advance preparation. Although theoretically grounded, it is designed to focus on the everyday instructional issues faced by bilingual teachers as they negotiate the linguistic, academic, and cultural considerations of their classrooms. The purpose of this book is to provide a hands-on practitioner's guide to the challenges of teaching in two languages to the ever-growing population of emergent bilingual students in our schools.

We have organized this book to easily provide you with the information needed to best serve your students. Each chapter begins with an overarching essential question—one that bilingual educators often ask. Thematically related subsections follow and are made more accessible through both vignettes that illustrate instructional dilemmas and solutions and through explicit ideas for instruction. The vignettes have been selected because of their power to engage the reader in thinking about critical instructional issues. The explicit instructional strategies are highlighted in sections titled "Try This!" Although they can be applied directly, they are meant for teachers to modify based on their individual context.

For ease in usage, Try This! activities are labeled with appropriate grade levels. Because the term *elementary* can designate different grade levels in different locales, for the purpose of uniformity we will use *lower elementary* to designate kindergarten through third grade and the term *upper elementary* to designate fourth through eighth grade. We have chosen to begin the upper elementary designation with the fourth grade because it is at Grade 4 that "learning to read" is generally recognized to segue into "reading to learn." In addition, we have provided for English as a second language/second language (ESL/L2) categories for each Try This! activity in Chapter 6, the chapter that focuses on second language instruction.

Although this book is meant to be a hands-on guide for practicing bilingual teachers, it may also be used as a supplemental text at the university level. For preservice teachers, we suggest that the Essential Question be used for weekly investigations within clinical settings. After researching an assigned question, preservice teachers can read the related chapter and compare what they have discovered to the corresponding content of the book.

Some commonly occurring questions of bilingual teachers are italicized in the paragraphs that follow; they are embedded in the corresponding chapters that address each one.

Chapter 1 focuses on language use in the bilingual classroom by posing the following essential question: *How do I use two languages in the bilingual classroom?* This is perhaps the most pressing question faced by bilingual teachers. While the use of two languages is implicit in bilingual education, educators are often unsure of how best to use them to the educational advantage of students. This chapter proposes that language use is best determined by program model as well as instructional goals and objectives, and that, even within this context, bilingual educators may choose from many appropriate instructional strategies.

Chapter 2 addresses culture, a topic that goes hand in hand with language. It asks, *Why does culture matter so much in the bilingual classroom?* Language and culture are intertwined. Thus, just as careful consideration must be given to the use of two languages, so too must consideration be given to the use of two or more cultures within the educational context. Even though bilingual programs are often labeled as *bilingual-bicultural,* in practice this is not always the case. In the over-crowded school curriculum, cultural considerations are often overlooked. This chapter emphasizes that bi- or multicultural classrooms can provide important supports for the academic success of bilingual students—supports that should not be disregarded.

Chapter 3 explicitly discusses curriculum and instruction in the native language. It asks, *Is teaching in a minority language really any different from teaching in English in a mainstream classroom?* If the answer to the question above were a simple "yes," there would be no need for this book. What, then, is the difference? We suggest that in addition to the linguistic and cultural considerations addressed in Chapters 1 and 2, providing a quality education to language-minority students demands moving away from the traditional transmission model of education and moving toward a constructivist stance.

Chapter 4 discusses bilingual curriculum and pedagogy specifically for content area instruction. It asks, *What approaches should teachers consider for teaching content to English language learners in bilingual classrooms?* In this examination of content area instruction, contributing author Irma M. Olmedo discusses teaching strategies for use in mathematics, science, and social studies, including techniques for emphasizing content vocabulary with emergent bilingual students.

Chapter 5 explores the following question: *How can I effectively develop vocabulary in the bilingual classroom?* Content area vocabulary is essential because it is the key to unlock the content itself. Unfortunately, many bilingual educators lack the technical vocabulary in the native language (L1) of their students that is necessary to effectively teach in the content areas of mathematics, science, and social studies. For these teachers, contributing author Jaime J. Gelabert-Desnoyer addresses content vocabulary and pedagogical vocabulary, including discussion of the impact of regional lexical variations. He describes the process of creating semantic maps, and he provides some as examples.

Chapter 6 discusses second language (L2) instruction, asking the question, *Do I need to have a separate time slot for teaching English as a second language?* Traditionally, ESL has been considered a separate subject that is often taught by ESL specialists in a pull-out program model. However, as more emphasis is placed on the integration of language and content learning, this practice is being called into question. This chapter addresses contemporary methods and strategies for teaching a second language.

Chapter 7 takes on the controversial role of assessment, asking, *How is assessment different in the bilingual classroom?* In this era of No Child Left Behind (NCLB), many educators are questioning a national overreliance on tests and asking if standardized tests are fair for ELLs. Assessment has come to be synonymous with standardized testing in the minds of many educators. Yet there are many other issues embedded in the topic of assessment for emergent bilingual students. This chapter not only discusses implications of NCLB for the instruction of ELLs, but also illuminates the multifaceted nature of assessment with bilingual students and provides examples of appropriate uses of assessment with ELLs that educators need not fear.

Chapter 8 expands the bilingual context by asking, *How can bilingual curriculum and instruction be applied to multiple learning contexts?* Bilingual education is adapting to a different political context and to the growing demand for opportunities for bilingual enrichment programs. While the primary audience for this book is teachers of ELLs in transitional and developmental programs of bilingual instruction, it contains implications for educators in a multitude of educational contexts that seek to provide educational opportunities for students to learn in two languages. In this chapter, we highlight the insights and suggestions of practicing bilingual educators as they offer guidance to teachers practicing in multiple language contexts, including private, religious, heritage, ESL, foreign language, and various immersion models. In an attempt to illuminate each teacher's authentic voice, we have not mandated conformity in terms of contribution length. Rather, the strength of each voice is reflected in the quality, not the quantity, of each educator's words.

Chapter 9, with its focus on equity and advocacy, goes to the heart of being a bilingual teacher: *How does being a bilingual teacher make me different?* It emphasizes collaboration with families for the benefit of students as essential to being a bilingual teacher, as well as discusses critical approaches to standardized testing.

Becoming a bilingual teacher requires additional professional preparation, not just in terms of language, but also in terms of curriculum and pedagogy. Bilingual teachers should be able teach in multiple contexts, from mainstream to multilingual classrooms. Yet bilingual teachers are often marginalized within public education just as bilingual education is often marginalized in the public eye. Contrary to such misperceptions, bilingual education is a multifaceted, multidisciplinary field, and bilingual teachers play a pivotal role in the quest for educational equity in this nation. Rather than being marginalized, they should be valued. This chapter highlights how being a bilingual teacher not only makes educators different, but also makes them important in ways that go beyond the world of the classroom.

Finally, **Chapter 10** summarizes the content of the book through vignettes that highlight stories of bilingual instruction. Through the words of both students and educators, we can see both the challenge and the promise of second language education.

Araceli, a practicing Spanish bilingual teacher, reflects on an instructional modification created for her bilingual learners.

> Before I do a mini-lesson, I do a mini-mini-lesson using visuals, building up their vocabulary, getting to see what experiences they had so that I can connect it to their writing and reading, and it has to be something they enjoy, too. So you have to look at where they come from, what are their experiences.

The purpose of this book is to empower you, the bilingual teacher, with knowledge that will assist you in doing just what Araceli has done—creating culturally and linguistically affirming educational environments in which students can grow developmentally and academically in two languages.

NOTE

1. In this book, we use both terms to refer to students who are adding the English language to their linguistic repertoire.

REFERENCES

Arce, J. (2004). Latino bilingual teachers: The struggle to sustain an emancipatory pedagogy in public schools. *International Journal of Qualitative Studies in Education, 17*(2), 227–246.

García, E. E. (2005). *Teaching and learning in two languages: Bilingualism and schooling in the United States.* New York: Teachers College Press.

García, E. E., & Cuellar, D. (2006). Who are these linguistically and culturally diverse students? *Teachers College Record, 108*(11), 2220–2246.

García, O., Kleifgen, J., & Falchi, L. (2007). *Equity in the education of emergent bilinguals: The case of English language learners.* Teachers College, Columbia University: Campaign for Educational Equity.

Ruíz-de-Velasco, J., Fix, M., & Clewell, C. B. (2000). *Overlooked and underserved: Immigrant students in U.S. secondary schools.* Washington, DC: The Urban Institute.

Acknowledgments

Thanks to Barb Bahner, Gloria Rahman, and Trina Vallone, whose support and encouragement from afar kept me writing as I completed a cross-country journey. Thanks, also, to Lena Baucum, Christine Decker Stone, Adria Dodici, Marta Villegas Gutiérrez, and the many others who created a warm and welcoming environment in which to complete this project.

—Sharon

I am grateful to my colleagues at The City College of New York, who have supported me in myriad ways. Specifically, I would like to thank Nancy Stern, a constant source of support, encouragement, and friendship, as well as Jesús Fraga, Soyong Lee, and Beverly Falk. I would also like to thank Michelle Boger, Christina Cepero, Kate Seltzer, Cristian Solorza, and my current and former students at City College, who have helped me explore ideas about being a bilingual teacher and, in one way or another, are a part of this book. I am especially indebted to Kate Menken and Tori Hunt for being the best colleagues and friends one could ask for. I also thank my parents, Fanya Mozeshtam and Jack Kleyn, for their unwavering love, as well as my sister, Beth Vayshenker, for her encouragement.

—Tatyana

We would first like to acknowledge the many amazing teachers that have contributed in various ways to this book. In particular we would like to thank Katherine Baldwin, Marilyn Balluta, Brigid Burke, Nelson Flores, Josie Freeman, Elizabeth Heurtefeu, Rebeca Madrigal, Melissa Marinari, Elizabeth Silva, Rabbi Ariel Stone, and Tulay Tashken for the valuable accounts of their work in Chapter 8. All have helped to paint a picture of what a bilingual teacher should aim for in an often contentious climate.

This work would not have been possible without the strong vision and unending support of Dan Alpert, our acquisitions editor, and Megan Bedell, who flawlessly managed to coordinate all the details.

From beginning to end, this book was a seamless collaborative project; it would not have been possible if we (Sharon and Tatyana) had not worked together so intensely. Working in this manner has not only been joyful, but it has enriched us both.

—Sharon and Tatyana

PUBLISHER'S ACKNOWLEDGMENTS

Corwin gratefully acknowledges the contributions of the following reviewers:

Todd Butler, Fourth Grade Bilingual Education Teacher
Erma Nash Elementary School, Mansfield, TX

TracyLynn Clark, Director I
English Language Learner Program, Clark County School District, Las Vegas, NV

Alberto Esquinca, Assistant Professor
Department of Teacher Education, University of Texas, El Paso

Elena Izquierdo, Associate Professor
Department of Teacher Education, University of Texas, El Paso

Christine Landwehrle, Fifth and Sixth Grade Reading and Language Arts Teacher
Bedminster Township Public School, Bedminster, NJ

Patty McGee, Professional Development Coach and Library Media Specialist
Harrington Park School, Harrington Park, NJ

Rachel Mederios, ELL Teacher
Jefferson Elementary, Meridian, ID

Maria D. Mercado, Associate Professor
Department of Curriculum & Instruction, New Mexico State University, Las Cruces, NM

Maria Mesires, Seventh Grade Life Science Teacher
Case Middle School, Watertown, NY

Kathleen Prisbell, Eighth Grade Language Arts Teacher
Russell O. Brackman Middle School, Barnegat, NJ

Carmen N. Zayas, Spanish Teacher
Brooklyn Prospect Charter School, Brooklyn, NY

About the Authors

 **Sharon Adelman Reyes** holds a PhD in Curriculum Design from the University of Illinois at Chicago, where she specialized in multicultural and bilingual education. A recipient of the Kohl International Prize for Exemplary Teaching, she was an elementary school teacher for twelve years and an elementary school principal for four years, prior to beginning her university career. She is currently an assistant professor at Gonzaga University, where she prepares graduate students for positions of educational leadership.

Sharon has published in peer-reviewed journals in the field of multicultural and bilingual education, has presented in her field locally, nationally, and internationally, and has served as an educational consultant in numerous school districts. Her current research agenda includes the preparation of educational leaders for diverse classrooms and educational contexts, and bilingual identity construction in schooling. Her first book, with co-author Trina Lynn Vallone, *Constructivist Strategies for Teaching English Language Learners* (2008), is also available through Corwin.

 **Tatyana Kleyn** is an assistant professor at The City College of New York in the Bilingual Education and TESOL (Teaching English to Speakers of Other Languages) program. In 2007, she received an EdD from Teachers College, Columbia University in International Educational Development, with a specialization in Bilingual/Bicultural Education. Her dissertation focuses on the intersections of bilingual and multicultural education in Spanish, Haitian Creole, Chinese, and Russian bilingual classrooms. In 2008, she received the second place Outstanding Dissertation Award from the National Association for Bilingual Education.

Tatyana is also an associate at the Research Institute for the Study of Language in Urban Society (RISLUS) at The Graduate Center in The City University of New York. There, she is involved in a multiphase study (with Kate Menken) that focuses on long-term English language learners in secondary schools. She has published in the United States and internationally about the cultural, linguistic, and educational needs of the Garífuna people in Honduras. She is currently working on a book for teenagers called *Immigration: Stories, Struggles, and Debates* (forthcoming from Scarecrow Press). Tatyana was an elementary school teacher in San Pedro Sula, Honduras, and Atlanta, Georgia.

About the Contributors

Jaime J. Gelabert-Desnoyer received his BA in Spanish Language and Literature at the University of the Balearic Islands in Mallorca, Spain; his MA in Spanish from the University of New Mexico; and his PhD in Spanish Applied Linguistics from The Pennsylvania State University in 2004. He taught Spanish and linguistics at Loyola University Chicago until 2009, when he accepted the position of Director of the Arcadia University Center for Catalan, Spanish, and Mediterranean studies. His research interests reside in the wider area of political discourse analysis, precisely pronominal forms and metaphoric language, as well as language pedagogy.

Irma M. Olmedo has been Associate Professor of Education at the University of Illinois Chicago. She has conducted research on children's bilingual development, oral histories of Latinas, issues of immigration and education, and the teaching of these subjects. Her work has been published in journals such as *Anthropology and Education Quarterly, Teaching and Teacher Education, Journal of Latinos and Education, Urban Education,* and *Qualitative Inquiry.*

1

Languages in the Bilingual Classroom

Essential Question

How do I use two languages in the bilingual classroom?

One Teacher's Dilemma

I went to one of the trainings where they were talking about teaching writing and reading. At the end we said, "You have been talking here about reading and writing, but we come from a dual language school and nobody here has talked about how to approach the teaching of reading and writing in Spanish." And her answer to our question was not to worry because she was going to translate her unit of study into Spanish, to which we responded that we knew how to read in English and didn't need a translation, that wasn't our question. So her view of teaching is that, well, I wrote a book about teaching reading and writing in English, and I will translate it and you should be able to teach it. And there are many differences with teaching any language or the approaches of teaching languages. You don't teach English the same way you teach Spanish or Russian; there are many things you must take into consideration. Don't tell me you're going to translate your book so I can buy it now in Spanish.

Dolores, a Spanish-English bilingual teacher, describes a common dilemma faced by bilingual educators. Oftentimes, the swift and insufficient response given to questions regarding the use of two languages in the classroom is to translate materials from English into the students' native language. This simplistic response fails to account for the multiple variables that bilingual teachers must consider when planning instruction and curriculum for their students. While the use of two languages is implicit in bilingual education, there appears to be little consensus as to how best to use the languages to the educational advantage of the students. This chapter proposes that language use is best determined by instructional goals and objectives and that, even within this context, bilingual educators may choose from many appropriate instructional strategies.

WORKING TOWARD LINGUISTIC EQUITY

The terms *equity* and *equality* are often used interchangeably, yet each word represents a different concept. In an educational context, *equality* translates to an equal distribution of resources for each child. However, we know that this would not be fair. It is necessary to allocate more resources to some students than to others. An equal education is not a fair education for all students because they come to school with different needs and different backgrounds. Children and youth with exceptionalities are a case in point. More resources are typically given to meet their special needs, and that does not seem to be up for debate. Yet when we talk about more and different educational resources being made available for emergent bilingual students, sensitivities are frequently raised. This is a reflection of the political climate in which we live. However, for English language learners (ELLs) to receive an equitable education, the needs of this subgroup must be carefully considered and fully met. In the words of Nieto and Bode (2008), "all students must be given the real possibility of an equality of outcomes" (p. 11).

How, then, do we ensure educational equity for bilingual students? Reyes and Vallone (2008, p. xi) suggest that the following components must be in place for this to occur:

1. Access to oral (communicative) English language development

2. Access to English language literacy

3. Access to academic content in English

4. Opportunities for cognitive development during academic instruction in English

5. Access to literacy in the native language

6. Access to academic content in the native language

7. Access to cognitive development in the native language

8. Access to understanding and functioning in the new culture

9. Maintenance of cultural and linguistic heritage

It is crucial to note that the first seven points are all directly related to language. The final two points are related to culture, and language and culture are inextricably intertwined. It is easy to see, then, how educational equity for bilingual students is fundamentally bound to issues of language.

A concept that is foundational to understanding how a second language develops is that it is necessary to differentiate between the conversational language needed for everyday communications and the formal, more scholarly language needed for academic success. Cummins (1994) named the former "Basic Interpersonal Communicative Skills (BICS)" and the latter "Cognitive/Academic Language Proficiency (CALP)." While BICS can develop in as little as two years, CALP requires a much longer period of time to be established; estimates range from five to nine years and depend on factors such as age, motivation, prior literacy, and academic development in the first language (L1). All students should, of course, develop CALP in their native tongue, and when they receive quality schooling in their country of origin or in the United States in their L1, this is the typical outcome. Things become more complex because of the need to hold the same expectation in the second language (L2).

TRY THIS!

Upper Elementary and Secondary Level

In order to have students distinguish between social and academic language (which can be a source of frustration for many socially fluent students when they feel like they know the language yet are still labeled as ELLs), have the class come up with a list of places where language is used. (Clearly, this list can be infinite, but get enough places to show variety.) It is likely that students will mention, for instance, the cafeteria, home, classroom, playground, or sporting events. Next, begin a conversation about the differences in social and academic language in English and the other language because this is a concept that is relevant in most languages. Then, have students work in pairs with two different colored pens or highlighters, using one color to represent social language and the other color to represent academic language. Have them highlight or underline which type of language is used in each setting, keeping in mind that it could be both. As a next step, students can work on translating sentences from social to academic language, or vice versa, to make them more appropriate for various situations.

The example below comes from Kate's 10th-grade English course. The class was reading *Nothing but the Truth,* by Avi, and also working on the genre of memo writing. Kate crafted a memo that emulates the language her students use in informal settings. The class was instructed to translate the original memo, which was directed at a character from the text. In Figure 1.1 you can see how Grisleysi, an intermediate ELL, used her knowledge of both social and academic language to translate the memo.

Figure 1.1

Name: _Grstafa S_ ~~~~~~~~~~~~

Unit 2: <u>Nothing but the Truth</u>

Date: _____

Points:

_____/10

<u>"YO MISS!" to "Dear Sir or Madam"</u>

Informal to Formal Language in Memo Writing

<u>Directions:</u>

1) **Discussion**: Differences between informal vs. formal language in writing

2) **Edits & Changes**: Informal to Formal Language – Read the memo below and, as a class, turn the slang (informal language) to professional language (formal language).

3) **Group Work**: At your tables, write a memo to our own principal about changes you would like to see at our school. You should focus on your own personal experiences at MACS and how relationships between teachers and students could be improved here.

<u>SAMPLE:</u>

— Dear, Dr. Doane

~~Yo Gertrude!~~
Good afternoon Doane, I wanted to tell you something.
~~What's up?~~ I wanted to talk to you about something. I think that the teachers at this school

be ~~beastin'~~ too much. They be yelling at us for no reason and they give us ~~mad~~ work. You
~~arguing~~ _Arguing_   _too much_
get mnow
really need to teach them to better understand us as students. They need to s~~pend some~~
our life & experiences outside of school.
~~time out on the streets and live in the 'hood for a little while.~~ ~~Don't worry, I'll make sure they~~

~~don't get jumped, LOL.~~ If you want I will give the teachers some lessons about our life so they
they don't give interest to the class in this days.
can make class more interesting because ~~it be MAD BORING~~. And then they be ~~blaming~~ us for
blame

~~wiling out!~~ _no paying attention and falling the class._
favor   ~~That I could help you~~
Let me know if you want me to do this for you. You know ~~I got your back. You just gotta pay~~
that I could help you
~~me a buck fity (naw I'm just playin you know I got you).~~ _w/ this._
any question just go to my class and I will be ther

Bobby Sanchez AKA Flaco
~~Sincerely,~~ _Sincerely, Bobby Sanchez_

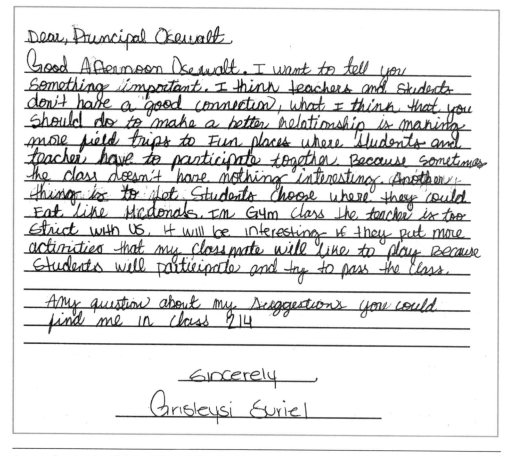

Dear, Principal Osewalt,

Good Afternoon Osewalt. I want to tell you something important. I think teachers and students don't have a "good" connection, what I think that you should do to make a better relationship is making more field trips to Fun places where students and teacher have to participate together. Because sometimes the class doesn't have nothing interesting. Another thing is to let students choose where they could Eat like Mcdonals. In Gym Class the teacher is too Strict with us, It will be interesting if they put more activities that my classmate will like to play Because students will participate and try to pass the class.

Any question about my suggestions you could find me in class 214

Sincerely,

Grisleysi Suriel

Source: Created by Grisleysi Suriel. Used with permission.

She then applied the distinctions to craft a memo to her own principal about how student-teacher relationships could be improved at her school.

This activity can be implemented as a way to scaffold the students' understanding of the differences in the ways varieties of one language are used in different settings. As a follow-up activity, students could also write their own piece in either social or academic language and have a peer translate it to make it a better fit for a specific context. Although the piece above requires students to work from social to academic language, working from academic to social or informal language is also important in order to show the value of both types of language.

With a basic understanding of educational equity for ELLs and the difference between BICS and CALP, we are ready to explore related linguistic issues that will take us to the heart of teaching in two languages in the K–12 classroom.

LANGUAGE EDUCATION PROGRAMS

Many programs fall under the large umbrella of bilingual education. Although these programs generally use two languages for instruction, their goals and implementation differ significantly. This book was written with the full range of bilingual programs in mind. First, we will briefly discuss ways of categorizing these programs. Next, we will succinctly explain each program type, since terminology changes across educational contexts and geographic locations. While we provide a fairly comprehensive listing of program types, this list is not meant to be exhaustive. In addition to variations on some models (for example, *immersion*), there are other programs that are not as prevalent (such as *newcomer programs*). Although understanding the foundational tenets of bilingual program models is an essential starting point, the main purpose of this volume is to provide information and guidance in bilingual *instruction;* therefore, we have limited this section.

A common way of categorizing programs for language learners is using the additive/subtractive distinction. *Additive* models have as their goal the maintenance of the native language and the addition of a second language. (In the United States, that second language is English.) *Subtractive* models are not concerned with the native language; the linguistic goal is proficiency in the second language. (Again, in the United States, that language would be English.) It is not uncommon for students enrolled in subtractive bilingual programs to eventually lose their native tongue, or to have it significantly weakened in comparison to English. Often the outcome of such programs in the United States is, thus, English monolingualism.

The additive and subtractive framework has dictated the ways in which bilingual programs have been categorized for many years. However, Ofelia García (2009) views this framework as somewhat limiting because it stems from a monolingual perspective, with the goal being either English monolingualism or bilingualism that is really "double monolingualism" (p. 52). This is because both languages are viewed as separate entities that function in isolation. To expand the possibilities and to better reflect the realities of programs that teach students in two or more languages, García has expanded the framework with two additional approaches: recursive and dynamic bilingualism. *Recursive bilingualism* is common in groups where the mother tongue is being brought back following oppressive policies and practices. Students are not learning a brand new language, but one that has existed to different degrees for generations; thus, there is a back and forth between language learning and loss. *Dynamic bilingualism* takes a departure from looking at two languages in isolation and refers to "a dynamic cycle where language practices are multiple and ever adjusting to the multilingual multimodal terrain of the communicative act" (García, 2009, p. 53). Therefore, languages are used in nonlinear ways to adjust to different needs and contexts. As programs continue to develop for our increasingly globalized world, it is likely that we will see models that address the recursive and dynamic bilingualism of our students.

As previously noted, our primary purpose in this book is not to provide an extensive discussion of models of bilingual and second language education. However, some understanding of such program models is necessary in order to provide not only instructional guidance but also conceptual insight into instruction in two languages. Accordingly, we will provide a basic synopsis of some of the most commonly described models of second language instruction.

Transitional models of bilingual instruction generally mandate percentages of the day for instruction in the L1 and the L2. These programs typically last no more than three years. Allowances for extended time in such programs vary from state to state and district to district. Typically, the L1 is used for instruction three-fourths of the time and the L2 is used one-fourth of the time during the first year a student is in the program. By the end of (usually) the third year in the program, this ratio has reversed, and students are typically exited from bilingual programs into mainstream English classrooms.

Developmental maintenance models of bilingual instruction may be stand-alone programs or may be extensions to transitional programs of instruction. As stand-alone programs, maintenance models may take the form of one-way developmental programs when the classroom is made up of ELLs. Maintenance models may function as extensions of transitional programs of instruction in contexts where educators realize the importance of native language development but lack the resources to provide extensive native language support over the years. In the latter situation, when students reach a level of English language proficiency sufficient for them to be exited from a transitional program of instruction, they may continue their literacy and content instruction in the L1 for a portion of the school day or week. Although instruction in and through the native language is strictly time limited, it does provide some continuity and L1 development in the bilingual education of students. Ramírez (1992) has termed this model as "late-exit transitional bilingual education" (p. 30).

English as a second language (ESL) programs provide additional support to students who are in the process of learning English. They are not generally thought of as a form of bilingual education, although they are often an integral part of bilingual programs. ESL strategies can be integrated into regular classroom instruction across the content areas, but often schools have ESL teachers who either pull out a group of students on a similar English level or push into mainstream classrooms to support the ELLs' English and content learning.

Immersion models come in various forms, both bilingual and monolingual. *Structured English immersion* is an all-English program for ELLs that is mandated in some states, in which bilingual education is largely forbidden. Yet immersion methodologies, such as sheltered English (also known as sheltered subject-matter instruction), are found in many bilingual programs as well. Certain foreign language and heritage language models also use immersion to foster the goal of bilingualism. In these "one-way" immersion programs, students from the same language background are taught primarily in another (target) language. Such models include Japanese and French immersion programs for English speakers in the United States and the Yup'ik heritage language program in Bethel, Alaska. Finally, two-way bilingual immersion (see below) is an approach in which students from two different groups develop proficiency in the other's language. The common thread is that immersion aims to teach the target language through content instruction in that language.

Two-way bilingual immersion (or *two-way dual language*) classes are developmental bilingual programs where the goals include bilingualism, biliteracy, academic achievement across the content areas, and cross-cultural understanding (Lindholm-Leary, 2001). More recently, Reyes and Vallone (2007) have suggested that identity construction is also a fundamental component of quality two-way bilingual immersion programs. At least 50% of instructional time is conducted in the language other than English (LOTE). Each class is divided (ideally in half) between English- and LOTE-dominant students. In some locations, this may be more of a continuum, with some students in the class entering at varying levels of bilingualism. Students' diversity may be evident not only in terms of ethnic or cultural heritage, but also in terms of other factors such as language dominance, race,[1] and class.

Heritage language programs are enrichment models intended for students who have exposure to another language and culture at home, but are not ELLs. While some students may be fluent in the LOTE, others may only have basic receptive skills. Heritage language programs take place during the school day, after regular school hours, or on weekends to reinforce students' connection to their native language and culture. Although these programs are sometimes limited in terms of their time allotment during the school day, they aim to develop and promote students' bilingualism and biculturalism. Two-way bilingual immersion programs often function as heritage language programs for language majority students with a language minority heritage. One-way bilingual or immersion programs can also function in this way when the target language is in danger of being lost to the individual or the community, for example, Yup'ik, Navaho, native Hawaiian, or French Creole in Louisiana.

Foreign language programs are generally required at the high school level, and they are offered less frequently at the middle school level (junior high school) and on occasion at the elementary school level. The number of years of foreign language study required for graduation varies and is dependent on state department of education regulations. Sometimes the study of a foreign language is begun at the middle school level, but this is usually by school or school district choice, not by mandate. Depending on the school district, students must either take the one foreign language offered at the school or select from a variety of offered languages. Foreign language classes are generally intended for students without prior exposure to that language, although some schools may offer heritage or advanced placement (AP) courses so that students with prior proficiency can be challenged and can build onto their linguistic skills (for example, "Spanish for Spanish speakers" classes). Foreign language programs generally meet for one period per day, and the goal over the years is for students to learn vocabulary, grammar, literacy, communication, and cultural elements associated with the language.

Before-school, after-school, or weekend foreign language programs on the elementary school level are designed to provide students with general exposure to a new language and culture. These programs engage students in hands-on activities, often through the arts, so that they can develop a basic vocabulary, learn how to engage in simple conversations, and develop an appreciation for a different culture. While some elementary foreign language programs may take a more traditional approach to language instruction, most aim to develop students' interest in becoming bilingual and multicultural individuals through participation in the culture being studied.

Religious or secular second language programs in private schools, also known as *enrichment models of language instruction*, cover a wide range of options, but are usually designed for children from a linguistic majority background. The majority of such programs take place within religious settings, such as the study of Hebrew within Jewish schools. However, some secular private schools offer foreign language instruction on the elementary level, and some even offer immersion schooling in languages such as French or Japanese.

NEGOTIATING ONE CLASSROOM AND TWO LANGUAGES

I haven't seen any textbooks, as such, like math. . . . I don't see any Chinese version. The only thing I've seen is they've translated one of the parent letters. So I have to juggle a lot because all the books are in English, so I have to use a bilingual math dictionary. . . . And in social studies, I haven't seen any books on the Civil War or American Revolution and things like that in Chinese. These are difficult books, but I don't see any books that are age-appropriate for my students.

Tung, a Chinese bilingual teacher, describes a common dilemma faced by bilingual teachers: the absence of content instructional materials in the native language of bilingual students. This problem is most typically seen in social studies and science (Lessow-Hurley, 2005), but as Tung notes, it occurs in math as well. Yet teaching in bilingual contexts can provide multiple opportunities for educators to refine their approaches to teaching and learning. Foremost among these opportunities is the possibility of maximizing the use of two classroom languages to meet social and instructional goals. How this is accomplished depends to a large extent on the program model endorsed by the school or school district. However, educators will also need to consider goals and objectives specific to the content being presented, as well as the linguistic strengths of students and families.

The use of two languages in an educational environment can enhance linguistic possibilities. Students can discover that they have expanded opportunities for self-expression, for understanding ideas from multiple perspectives, and for accessing information. Unfortunately, rather than viewing bilingualism as an enhanced way of viewing and interacting with the world, educators and parents sometimes worry about language confusion. Yet when bilingual instructional strategies are thoughtfully planned and carried out, language confusion need not be a concern. Even young children sort out the difference between languages when allowed a developmentally appropriate amount of time. In educational contexts, this natural childhood tendency to differentiate between languages (Hakuta, 1986) can be assisted and reinforced.

When planning for bilingual instruction, program model is a primary consideration. Both two-way bilingual immersion, also known as *dual language programs*, and developmental bilingual education integrate language and content learning in order to teach both simultaneously. For example, students might learn English through science and Spanish through social studies. Because language and literacy are developed through content, both models usually maintain a strict separation of language by content area. Biliteracy is also developed strictly in the L1 or in the L2. This language separation is primarily for instructional purposes.

However, at appropriate instructional moments, it is all right—and even encouraged—to make connections across languages.

In other bilingual programs, this strict linguistic separation is less common. Transitional bilingual models, for example, tend to be more flexible in the use of two languages for instructional purposes. In our experience, the lack of clarity regarding language use in transitional programs can encourage problematic practices, such as repeating instruction in one language that has already been given in another (content transfers across languages) and using translation and random, unplanned language mixing and code switching. While we are not uniformly opposed to mixing two languages in the classroom, when it occurs it should be the result of purposeful planning in order to achieve specific goals and objectives. Sometimes, teaching bilingually may be essential. For example, while students can master content faster in their native language, if they do not also learn content vocabulary in English, they will be at a tremendous disadvantage when facing standardized achievement tests. It is important to remember that while content easily transfers from the L1 to the L2, vocabulary may not transfer without explicit instruction. For this reason, specific techniques have been developed for deliberately teaching content bilingually in a structured and purposeful manner.

TRY THIS!

Upper Elementary and Secondary Level

In the *Preview-Review strategy* (Lessow-Hurley, 2005), also known as *Preview-View-Review,* content is previewed in one language, taught in another, and then reviewed in the first language. Thus, the linguistic instructional pattern would be either L1-L2-L1 or L2-L1-L2. Try this technique using an upper elementary or secondary text on the American Civil War, a topic most suitable for these grades. Use a KWL (Know, Want to Know, Learned) strategy in the L1 to explore what the students already know about this seminal event in U.S. history. Highlight key vocabulary. Use texts in the L2 to let students discover what more they want to know about the American Civil War. For example, was it really fought over the issue of slavery, or was it primarily about economics? Then, hold a discussion in the L1 to highlight student discoveries. Note that it is important that this remains an instructional activity focused on brainstorming, reading, sharing, and discussing information and points of view. If the teacher uses context and cognate clues during the L2 portion of the activity, student prior knowledge can be effectively tapped. *Note that if the teacher were to change the focus of this activity to that of writing a research paper, it would become an exercise in translation, which is not a recommended practice.*

In general, the use of two languages should be specifically planned for instructional purposes. There are times, however, when it makes good instructional sense to allow students to speak to each other bilingually during planned classroom activities. If the instructional goal is purely mastery of content, there is little need to control the language of conversation. For example, if students are conducting a scientific experiment in cooperative groups in order to discover a scientific principle, the language of communication between them makes little difference. Once concepts are discerned, however, educators will need to ensure that students have the appropriate vocabulary to explain such concepts in the L1, the L2, or both.

To determine how to teach in bilingual contexts, it is important to determine the programmatic and instructional goals and objectives. If an educational activity has both linguistic and content goals, it is best to stick to the use of one language. If, on the other hand, there are only content goals for a given activity, language choice becomes less relevant. However, it is rarely the case that language and content goals do not go together. In the bilingual classroom, virtually every content lesson should also be a language lesson. It is good to keep in mind that even in mainstream, English-only classrooms, we often talk about teaching reading across the curriculum.

The prevalent thought in literacy instruction is to use the L1 as a bridge to the L2. In subtractive program models for ELLs, once literacy is achieved in the L2, the L1 is disregarded. In additive programs of bilingual instruction, the L1 is maintained and developed. Dual language programs in places such as New York City frequently teach literacy simultaneously in English and Spanish in order to avoid the controversial nature of teaching initial literacy in Spanish in the current political climate.

SELECTING EDUCATION RESOURCES IN TWO LANGUAGES

The selection of books and other educational materials should depend on the curriculum. Unfortunately, in classrooms based on a transmission model of instruction, textbooks often drive the curriculum. We strongly believe that curriculum decisions should be the domain of the teacher. Here are some principles that may assist educators in their deliberations over appropriate educational materials for bilingual contexts.

When the objective is teaching language and content simultaneously, the choice is clear. Educational materials should be selected in the target language, whether it be the L1 or the L2. This is the case in immersion and maintenance (developmental) program models. However, the choice is less clear when lessons are not as language specific or during times when students have free choice. For example, educators should give considerable thought to their own classroom library. In addition to the usual concerns of readability, interest level, illustrations, organization, multicultural representation, and layout, bilingual educators must decide if they prefer books in the L1, the L2, or a combination of both. Clearly, it is good to encourage reading in both languages. A more difficult question has to do with bilingual books, which are typically available in a variety of formats. Sometimes, it is best to avoid those that have text in both the L1 and the L2 on the same page, or two adjacent pages, because the reader will be inclined to read the text in his or her dominant language since that is easier and more natural. It is preferable to order separate copies of picture and chapter books in the L1 and the L2 if the explicit instructional purpose is to read in a particular language. In this manner, the teacher can make instructionally-based decisions about which books to display to which students at any given time. Yet in some situations, children can be taught how to use bilingual books effectively in order to compare the two languages and to independently further their own language learning. Of course, some bilingual books code switch purposefully. In this case, children can learn that languages do not always appear in isolation and that language mixing does occur.

Books with a bilingual presentation come in a variety of formats. When the text is displayed simultaneously in both languages, it may be divided by color (e.g., black font vs. red font), placement (one language on the top, the other on the bottom, or one on the right, the other on the left), or a combination of both. Less common, but more effective, are picture books that have an entire story first in one language, then in the other. Such a format is helpful with children who are motivated to purposefully promote their own bilingualism. When reading in their L2, such children can go to the corresponding page in their L1 to check on the meaning of an unknown phrase.

Videos, DVDs, and audio recordings can be used to enhance instruction given in either the L1 or L2 or to augment instruction in one language with the same concepts in another. This concept parallels the Preview-Review strategy by presenting similar content in separate linguistic segments. It is not redundant because it is not a translated activity but rather a supplemental one to reinforce concepts already learned and to provide bilingual vocabulary development.

TRY THIS!

Secondary Level

Have trade books on global warming and related environmental issues written in the L1 available in the classroom. After small-group or full-class discussion, show a portion of the film *An Inconvenient Truth.* Afterward, ask students to be on the alert for any newspaper or magazine articles that they might find in either the L1 or the L2 on the same topic and highlight them on a bilingual bulletin board. Be especially diligent about searching out information that impacts the geographic location of your school and community. Invite a speaker from the local Public Health Department to speak to the class regarding environmental concerns in your own community. (This can be in the L1 or in the L2, depending on the personnel available through the corresponding agency.) Structure a classroom activity around a relevant environmental issue. When involving the community, this activity might take place in the L2. Many objectives can be achieved, including those related directly to science content, language learning, and the affective domain. In addition, students can be guided into seeing concretely how bilingualism can be an asset in both uncovering information and in community improvement. Access to two languages gives access to more informational sources and perspectives and to the possibility for greater community involvement.

Technology and learning games may be used in the same manner, either to reinforce concepts in the same language as the original instruction or to assist in vocabulary development and provide essential background information that makes the L2 more comprehensible. The use of technology is not only expanding; it is essential in order to prepare students for many aspects of life. (See Gee, 2003, for more on technology and games.)

THE LIMITED ROLE OF TRANSLATION

Translation is a distinct skill—complicated, complex, and difficult. The goal of bilingual education, at least additive bilingual education, is not to produce translators, but to propel students toward fluency and critical literacy in two languages. In other words, our goal should be to empower students to fully function intellectually, socially, academically, and cognitively in their L1 and their L2. Of course, the ability to translate across languages to some extent may be a natural by-product of bilingualism, but it is not a primary instructional goal. Educators would be well advised to avoid instructional activities that many inadvertently turn into translation exercises. For example, if Spanish is being taught through a social studies unit on the Aztecs, and as a final project the students are required to produce a written research report in Spanish on an aspect of life in the Aztec empire, it would be ill advised to have the students gather research material from trade books written on this topic in English. The final project would thus become an exercise in translation because students would have to gather information in English and write their findings in Spanish. If trade books and other resource materials on the Aztecs were unavailable in Spanish, this type of final project would not be consistent with the goals of a bilingual curriculum. If educators have student creation of a research paper in Spanish as an objective, one criterion to consider would be on what topics materials in Spanish could be obtained. In the activity described previously, the study of the Aztecs might best be accomplished in English, or with a different type of design and final product.

All of this should not imply that it is never appropriate to translate within the bilingual classroom. Although it is generally best to define unknown words in the same language through description, explanation, and context (just as mainstream teachers explain unknown English words in English), there may be times when lengthy descriptions could inhibit instructional flow. Idioms might also be more readily understood if a counterpart exists in the second language. And of course, in urgent situations, the quickest way to communicate is always best. Yet for the most part, translation is counterproductive. A learner's natural tendency is to tune out the more difficult language and to tune in the more familiar.

TRY THIS!

Elementary and Secondary Level

Have students generate a theme they are interested in. On a trip to the library, let each student find a book on this theme at an appropriate reading level and in the language of his or her choice. Follow up by facilitating several full-class discussions on the theme, rotating language and avoiding redundancy.

USING CODE SWITCHING FOR INSTRUCTION

Code switching, or "the alternate use of two languages from sentence to sentence, or even within one sentence" (Lessow-Hurley, 2005, p. 38), is often mistaken for linguistic confusion or the lack of proficiency in a given language. Linguists, however, have rejected this interpretation and favor one that sees code switching in most situations as an indication of linguistic vitality, creativity, and fluidity—thus, a normal extension of bilingualism. Common reasons for code switching include filling a lexical need (such as a word used in one language that does not have an equivalent counterpart), emphasizing a point (by repeating it in another language), and expressing ethnic solidarity (Lessow-Hurley, 2005; Olmedo, 2005).

Code switching may occur naturally in the classroom as a result of heightened emotion, as a sign of affection between teacher and student, or because a particular word may not exist in another language (e.g., names for indigenous artifacts or religious concepts). Previously, it was generally agreed that when code switching occurred, the inter-sentential (switching between sentences) variety was preferable to the intra-sentential (switching within a sentence) variety (Lessow-Hurley, 2005). However, this line of thinking is being called into question. Zentella (1997) argues that intra-sentential switching may be a more sophisticated and skillful process than inter-sentential switching since speakers have to abide by the grammatical structure of both languages.

Bilingual poetry is a genre that not only builds identity and gives voice to bilingual students, but also doubles their expressive and rhyming possibilities. It demonstrates the creative and purposeful use of code switching within a literary context and is thus an acceptable form of code switching in the bilingual classroom. Ada (2003) lists many examples of bilingual poetry books. Bilingual poetry collections are becoming increasingly popular and can be obtained easily through numerous publishers and bookstores.

TRY THIS!

Elementary and Secondary Level

Provide language frames (Rosaen, 2003) or stems for students, such as "I am from...." Use the stem repeatedly, letting the students finish the sentences in their native language. For example, a place (*un lugar*), a favorite food (*comida preferida*), a favorite color (*color favorito*), a favorite activity (*algo que te gusta hacer*), and so forth. The finished poems will feature English stems and creative endings in the L1. Students can share their poems and discuss how bilingual poetry helps define who they are.

USING THE ARTS FOR BILINGUALISM AND BILITERACY

The creative arts have long been recognized as having an inherently motivational impact on student learning. Perhaps this lies in the nature of the arts as a vehicle for self-expression of the human spirit. The creative arts are a logical part of childhood curriculum, where play is seen as a primary force for learning. The creative arts should also be a logical part of curriculum for youth, where self-expression is an extension of the search for identity—which is a primary force for learning at that level. Because drama is the art form that relies most heavily on the spoken word, it is a natural and logical extension of the linguistic curriculum of the classroom. It is also the art form that most easily draws upon elements of all other art forms within an educational context. Movement and dance, rhythm and music, crafts and visual arts, and poetry and other forms of creative writing all flow seamlessly from creative (educational) drama. Unfortunately, in an era that is so dominated by standardized tests and formal assessments, this potent vehicle for language learning has been largely left behind in the public and educational discourse. It is our purpose here to present an alternate vision for the use of the creative arts, one where drama is used as a base and is an integral part of a classroom in two languages.

Creative drama (the use of drama as an educational process) has traditionally been used in monolingual classroom contexts. Creative instructors also typically use elements of theater as a tool for reinforcing second language learning in foreign language contexts. What we espouse here is a way of using drama that incorporates elements of both creative drama and more formal theater.

Bilingual teachers have the advantage of using two languages in the education of their students. With this comes the responsibility of clear and careful thought. What language is to be used, and for what purpose? Teaching through the arts in the bilingual classroom is no different. As an example, we discuss how the bilingual teacher might approach improvisational techniques. We hope to illuminate the purposeful thought that goes into planning drama activities in a bilingual classroom so that teachers might emulate this thinking in planning other drama activities.

Improvisation is used frequently in educational drama classrooms. More so than scripted dramatizations, it forces both critical and creative thought. Rather than relying on memorization, students must decide what a given character might say and do in a given situation. Ironically, a by-product of this process-oriented approach to drama is oftentimes a better theatrical product. When students are able to think for themselves, their presentations may be more honest and realistic. Rather than "playing at" being a character, they are internalizing aspects of that character. However, while improvisation thus poses many benefits in the monolingual classroom, it poses special challenges in a second language classroom when drama is also being used as a technique for language learning. (In this sense, it is the integration of language and content, with the L2 as the language and drama as the content.) Students who might otherwise be thoroughly engaged in creating characters, scenes, and situations might be rendered voiceless due to lack of second language proficiency. Teachers might be tempted to go back to scripted dialogs that easily become stilted and dry. Using Readers Theater as a bridge to improvisation can accomplish multiple objectives. This genre of educational theater is meant primarily to illuminate and give voice to literature. Although scripted, it should not be memorized. In fact, keeping a script in hand in front of an audience is required in this genre because it illuminates the power of the written word to the audience. Yet because the script is meant to be powerfully interpreted, it must be rehearsed repeatedly. (Choral reading arrangements can function in much the same way.) Multiple repetitions serve the purpose of reinforcing both syntax and vocabulary for second language learners. In this sense, the script may be used as a scaffold to an improvised production of the same literary piece. Costumes and props should be symbolic, thus minimizing their importance. So, too, should a minimalist approach be used with *blocking,* or the choreography of a play. These are purposeful techniques, used to emphasize the power of the written word. As a follow-up activity to a formal Readers Theater production, second language learners could improvise scenes from the literary work. This would give them a chance to more fully interpret the characters they are portraying, while at the same time allowing them to practice new language patterns and vocabulary. In addition to second language learning, then, students are engaged in literature study through the motivational means of drama. Language learning has been scaffolded through Readers Theater.

TRY THIS!

Upper Elementary and Secondary Level

Typically, a second language teacher might have beginning second language students construct menus for a fictional restaurant as a way of teaching vocabulary related to food. A common follow-up activity is to have the students role-play the diners and waitstaff. For intermediate and advanced second language students, this activity could be extended by giving each student an index card a day in advance with "secret" information. Index cards could hold instructions such as the following:

"You left home without breakfast and have not eaten in seven hours. You are feeling ill from hunger."

"Your shift should have ended two hours ago, but the restaurant is short-staffed and you are not able to leave yet."

Make sure students have the resources to obtain the targeted language patterns and vocabulary to enact their role. This might include time set aside with students or school staff who are native speakers of the L2. The ensuing dramatization might be repeated several times to both perfect performance and provide L2 language reinforcement. Final enactments could be performed for the class, or transcribed into a script for another group of students within the classroom, so that all students could have access to the same language patterns and vocabulary.

READ ALOUDS IN BILINGUAL SETTINGS

Reading aloud is a salient part of literacy, and even content instruction, from the early to the secondary grades. There are myriad reasons to read literature to students, including exposure to text structures across genres, an increase in vocabulary acquisition, modeling pronunciation, development of comprehension skills, and access to higher-level books (Edwards-Santoro, Chard, Howard, & Baker, 2008; Hickman, Pollard-Durodola, & Vaughn, 2004). Read alouds also provide spaces for students to use their cultural backgrounds to interpret, challenge, and form connections to the text. Fanya, a Russian bilingual teacher, explains how her class incorporated their prior experiences during a read aloud of a historical fiction book. The author, of Eastern European descent, incorporates her family's experiences into her stories:

> She was born and raised here [in the United States], has little knowledge [about Eastern Europe], and sometimes you can see how it's fake a little bit, because she doesn't have these roots. . . . Maybe she kind of reinvents different things. That's why we go back to our ancestors and say if you ask your grandmother to write a story, it will be more primary in terms of resources and historical background.

Read alouds look different based on the type of bilingual program and the grade-level one teaches. Dual language teachers have a firm division of languages that makes navigating books and languages challenging. In this section, we will outline two structures proposed by María Torres-Guzmán to ensure continuity of books, languages, and content during read alouds in a dual language setting.

The first structure is the Alternate Language Read Aloud (ALRA) (Torres-Guzmán, 2005). This approach requires that the text be available in the LOTE and in English. One day the teacher reads a chapter or portion of the book in one language, and the next day the book is continued in the second language. There is no repetition of the section read the prior day, although a brief review is certainly important. This approach has several benefits. Students who are weak in one language will benefit from hearing at least half of the book in their L1. In addition, there is a strong opportunity to teach for transfer, as students will develop understanding of concepts in their native language and then continue their development in the L2. Finally, ALRA allows teachers to read longer chapter books to students without having interruptions due to the language of the day. The drawbacks are that many books are not available in different languages, and, when they are, the translations are often inauthentic and inaccurate.

Translated versions of books are often from English to the LOTE, rather than vice versa. This one-way translation can inadvertently eliminate the perspectives of cultural groups represented by the LOTE.

The second structure is referred to as Parallel Read Aloud (PRA) (Torres-Guzmán, 2005). Instead of using the same book in two languages, teachers select two different books that usually come from one genre, address the same topic, and work to meet the same learning objective. Often, these books are shorter in length so that they can be read in one period. This structure allows for a wider selection of books across languages and topics, the inclusion of authentic literature, and multiple perspectives. However, PRA is more challenging for students at the early stages of second language development because they only have access to the text in one language. This approach may also be limiting due to the use of shorter books, and switching between read aloud books every day may be confusing and inconsistent.

TRY THIS!

Upper Elementary and Secondary Level

Select a book that has a translation available to read aloud. As you alternate between books, using the ALRA structure, have students pay attention to discrepancies in relation to language use, culture, and overall meaning. Chart these inconsistencies in each language as you read. Once you've completed the book, have students write about the advantages and disadvantages of translated texts. This will help students develop a critical eye and be open to challenging what they encounter in print, rather than accepting it blindly.

Although read alouds are typically associated with primary grades, they are effective and important at the secondary level as well. At the upper levels, read alouds offer opportunities for language learners to be exposed to fluency and comprehension strategies that are made explicit during think alouds. Teachers can read short passages and stop at various points in order to make explicit how experienced readers approach challenging vocabulary, focus on a grammatical structure, make predications and subsequent confirmations, and summarize chunks of text as they read (Calderón, 2007). Think alouds within read alouds model and uncover strategies that are often expected of students but are never taught to them in explicit ways.

Whether you are a secondary content teacher or a first-grade dual-language teacher, read alouds are effective in teaching content, language, and strategies to all students. As a bilingual teacher, it's important to determine not only the book you will read, but how it addresses content and language objectives. Therefore, careful planning through prereading is critical to make read alouds an effective part of instruction.

Return to the Essential Question

How do I use two languages in the bilingual classroom?

Decisions about language choice in bilingual classrooms depend on a wide variety of factors, including program type, goals and objectives of the unit or lesson, availability of resources, and student needs and backgrounds. Choices about isolating versus comparing versus mixing languages add yet another layer of complexity to this chapter's essential question. While there is no one clear response to the question we pose, every program and every teacher need to develop a comprehensive language-allocation plan that outlines how languages are to be used and the reason for such decisions. On a smaller scale, each lesson's language choices should also be calculated to provide students with a sound bilingual education that allows them to become bilingual and biliterate individuals.

One Teacher's Response

Gerard, a Haitian Creole bilingual teacher, explains how he perceives the interplay of languages for communication:

> I encourage them (the students) to use any language because culturally, explaining something in one language is easier or makes more sense. Because you can translate something and even if you're really proficient in both languages, it's not the same.

For bilingual teachers and students, language is the key to opening up words and worlds. In the next chapter, we will explore the power of culture to do the same.

NOTE

1. The concept of race has been called into question as a social construct.

REFERENCES

Ada, A. F. (2003). *A magical encounter: Latino children's literature in the classroom.* New York: Pearson Education.

Calderón, M. E. (2007). *Teaching reading to English language learners, grades 6–12: A framework for improving achievement in the content areas.* Thousand Oaks, CA: Corwin.

Cummins, J. (1994). Primary language instruction and the education of language minority students. In California State Department of Education, *Schooling and language minority students: A theoretical framework* (2nd ed., pp. 3–46). Los Angeles: Evaluation, Dissemination, and Assessment Center, California State University.

Edwards-Santoro, L., Chard, D. J., Howard, L., & Baker, S. K. (2008). Making the very most of classroom read-alouds to promote comprehension and vocabulary. *The Reading Teacher, 61*(5), 396–408.

García, O. (2009). *Bilingual education in the 21st century: A global perspective.* West Sussex, United Kingdom: Wiley-Blackwell.

Gee, J. P. (2003). *What video games have to teach us about learning and literacy.* New York: Palgrave, MacMillan.

Hakuta, K. (1986). *Mirror of language: The debate on bilingualism.* New York: Basic Books.

Hickman, P., Pollard-Durodola, S., & Vaughn, S. (2004). Storybook reading: Improving vocabulary and comprehension for English language learners. *The Reading Teacher, 57,* 720–730.

Lessow-Hurley, J. (2005). *The foundations of dual language instruction.* New York: Pearson.

Lindholm-Leary, K. (2001). *Dual language education.* Clevedon, England: Multilingual Matters.

Nieto, S., & Bode, P. (2008). *Affirming diversity: The sociopolitical context of multicultural education.* New York: Pearson.

Olmedo, I. M. (2005). The bilingual echo: Bilingual children as language mediators in a dual language school. In M. Farr (Ed.), *Latino language and literacy in ethnolinguistic Chicago.* Mahwah, NJ: Erlbaum.

Ramírez, J. D. (1992). Executive summary. *Bilingual Research Journal, 16,* 1–62.

Reyes, S. A., & Vallone, T. L. (2007). Toward an expanded understanding of two-way bilingual immersion education: Constructing identity through a critical, additive bilingual/bicultural pedagogy. *Multicultural Perspectives 9*(3), 3–11.

Reyes, S. A., & Vallone, T. L. (2008). *Constructivist strategies for teaching English language learners.* Thousand Oaks, CA: Corwin.

Rosaen, C. (2003). Preparing teachers for diverse classrooms: Creating public and private spaces to explore culture through poetry writing. *Teachers College Record, 105*(8), 1437–1485.

Torres-Guzmán, M. E. (2005). La lecture suivie n'est-elle *qui* lecture suivie? (Are read alouds *just* read alouds?). *Lettre de l'AIRDF (International Research Association in French Didactics),* No. 25, 98–108.

Zentella, A. C. (1997). *Growing up bilingual: Puerto Rican children in New York.* Malden, MA: Blackwell.

2 Cultures in the Bilingual Classroom

Essential Question

Why does culture matter so much in the bilingual classroom?

One Teacher's Dilemma

The first-grade students come into the classroom, put their belongings away, and gather on the carpet. The teacher engages the class in a conversation regarding their understanding of the events that will occur in the month of March:

Ms. Sanchez:	So it's March and María's birthday. Let's look and see (pointing to the calendar).
Juan (eagerly raising his hand):	I know what March is; it has leprechauns, some gold pots, and rainbows.
Ms. Sanchez:	What else do we know about the month of March?
Tamara:	A rainbow comes, sun showers.
Armando:	St. Patrick's Day, you make cards shaped like clovers.

Does this sound familiar? It's likely that this scenario does not strike you as something different or out of the ordinary for an elementary classroom. It is also possible that this scene will play itself out over and over again during the upcoming years as these first graders move through the elementary school curriculum. This vignette demonstrates the prevalence of a one-sided approach toward culture in the classroom. While teachers try to bring in different holidays to expose students to a range of events and cultures, those most commonly taught stem from the Euro-American traditions that are entrenched in the U.S. school system—and even such holidays may be trivialized by a shallow approach. For example, by the first grade, students have a superficial knowledge of an often-celebrated Irish holiday, St. Patrick's Day. They can identify all the symbols associated with it, but they cannot explain the meaning behind them or the holiday itself. Yet this is an important religious holiday that has been celebrated by the Irish for thousands of years. The lack of depth in teaching about it not only deprives students of Irish descent from accessing their own cultural heritage, but denies *all* children an understanding of an important part of human history.

If we think back to our own schooling, many of us will find that we are products of a "holidays and heroes" approach and are predisposed to falling into the same patterns. However, by being more aware of how we address cultures, both those present and absent from the classroom, we can provide our students with a more holistic and diverse education. This chapter looks at how to begin instruction from students' cultural backgrounds and then move outward so that students are exposed to diversity, whether it is present in the school or not.

CULTURAL CONSIDERATIONS IN THE BILINGUAL CLASSROOM

In the United States, the mainstream culture is what is primarily valued and, thus, included within the curriculum. Individuals from white, upper-middle-class, Standard English speaking backgrounds generally fall within this group. These societally dominant characteristics often differ drastically from the characteristics of students in bilingual classrooms. Due to the mismatch between the culture most recognized in the school and the culture represented in the students' homes, teachers must pay special attention to how and whose cultures are present and absent within the classroom.

María analyzes why her Iraqi (Kurdish and Arabic) students were not initially achieving academically in the classroom. She foregrounds cultural considerations:

It was . . . likely that the Iraqi students were not learning because they could not participate meaningfully in the Western thought-based curriculum that was not only linguistically but also culturally alien to them. U.S. public school curriculum is derived from the beliefs, norms, and expectations, and general knowledge base shared by the middle class not only in the United States but also throughout most of the Western world. The Western thought paradigm, which merges Judeo-Christian values with an evidence-based approach to scientific knowledge, is difficult for non-Westerners to access, especially if they lack formal education and have not been exposed to Western culture. All of the failing Iraqi students had experienced interruptions in their schooling due to their families' flight from war zones into refugee camps and their subsequent resettlement. Because of such disruptions, some of the children had never had a chance to attend school at all. Moreover, many had come from farming communities in which the level of education was minimal. (Reyes & Vallone, 2008, p. 108)

But what exactly do we mean by *culture*, a term that is often pigeonholed with artifacts such as food, holidays, dance, and traditional clothing. These are all certainly aspects of culture, but if we consider these the most important or only parts of a given culture, we will find ourselves stuck in a "holidays and heroes" approach. As the vignette at the beginning of this chapter illustrates, that often provides our students a superficial and stereotypical understanding of a limited number of cultural groups. We can expand our definition of culture, however, to include the ways in which issues or problems are approached, family structures, and the roles and intersections of age, sex, class, and gender. We can begin to focus on deep culture (e.g., value systems) rather than surface culture (e.g., food, clothing). For example, Rosario, a fifth grade bilingual teacher, explains that in her classroom "we always talk about how do you do it in your country or how do you say it in your country?" She validates different cultures and even different varieties of languages, while at the same time bringing in new material. This broadening of the term allows us to include these areas as a natural part of instruction. In other words, we do not need to wait for a particular holiday or to hold a special event where students bring in a typical dish to learn about, compare, and even critique cultures.

This is not to say, however, that holidays or special events should completely be overlooked. Following is an example of an assembly that pushed students and their audience to get at the crucial issues associated with Haitian independence and the events that followed:

The auditorium is filled on a hot June day with students and parents for the morning performance of the Haitian Flag Day celebration (which comes a month after the actual holiday). Students from various classes perform skits, poems, and dances to commemorate Haiti's culture and history. Students take part in a skit that brings students back to the Battle of Vertières and its role in bringing Haitians freedom from the French. A girl plays a wise mother who tells a story to her children about the enslavement of blacks in Haiti and the victorious battle that followed. "We're free!" chant the students. Next, students explain how they can show love for their country. Some advice includes, "In unity comes strength, we won't let anyone take advantage of our country. Haiti is a poor country; let's not forget the people are equally our brothers and sisters. Remember Haiti is our country, even though we are living abroad, you have to contribute to development, never forget that is where you come from." Students come out with teachers in traditional, colorful clothes to do partner dances. Finally, a girl comes to the stage to read a poem that comes back to the stanza, "If we forget, who will remember?" The MC comes on the microphone and enthusiastically announces, "YOU SEE HOW THEY DO IT IN HAITI. IT'S A HAITI PARTY!!" The crowd erupts into applause and cheers.

All the Haitian bilingual teachers collaborated to put together this annual event in order to remind all students (regardless of background) of Haitian history, culture, and traditions. In addition to portraying historical events, students were encouraged to remain active in their country, which still faces an uphill battle against poverty and corruption. Both the positive and more difficult aspects of the cultural group were presented to provide a holistic picture. This pushed students to think in critical ways about culture, instead of staying within a "sunny side-up" approach that glosses over areas of injustices (Nieto, 2002).

As the vignette demonstrates, when we think about and teach about culture, we need to go beyond "how it was." We can also consider how it is now and how it is changing. We should avoid the trap of viewing culture from a traditional perspective (from our grandparents' days) and failing to look at present day culture and how it has evolved over time. Culture, like language, is constantly changing, especially in our interconnected world where technology allows different groups to connect as never before.

USING NATIVE CULTURE TO ENHANCE LEARNING

For learning to occur, teachers need to start with what students know; that is, we must consider their strengths. Every student comes to school with a home culture, and using background as a focal point in the curriculum can be powerful. This is the concept of *centricity* (Asante, 1991). Students' cultural groups are placed in a central position so that they can understand and appreciate their own backgrounds before they develop an understanding and appreciation of the backgrounds of other cultural groups, dominant and nondominant alike. Centricity is a concept that combines culture and pedagogy. Learning is primarily about making connections between concepts and ideas, rather than memorizing isolated facts. When we start from our students' backgrounds and understandings and move outward, they are able to learn in more meaningful ways.

As an example, a Chinese bilingual teacher explains how she approaches a unit on the United States from the centric perspective of her Chinese immigrant students:

> Based on the curriculum, we study America for the first few months; so we talk about the new country and why we came here. I touch on their backgrounds. I ask them, do you know, do you have any idea why you are here in America? You were in China. So we talk about them, and then we talk about [how] you can go home and talk to Mommy and Daddy about what are the reasons they came here.

In order to begin from students' cultural and linguistic backgrounds, the teacher must first gather at least a basic understanding of the groups within her class. One benefit of being a bilingual teacher is that you speak at least two of the languages of your students, and the languages serve as an opening for different cultural knowledge. As we learn about our students, we should remember that this is the perfect opportunity for them to be our teachers. This does not mean we cease seeking information on our own, but that we take a multipronged approach to learning about our students and their individual backgrounds.

There are, however, a few areas we need to be careful about when we classify students into cultural groups. First, we cannot assume that just because a student comes from a given background that she or he will necessarily fall within that group's general characteristics. For example, a student from China may struggle with learning math in spite of the "model minority" stereotype. Naturally, we need to know children as individuals, remaining cognizant of the fact that variations exist within and across cultural groups. When we consider overarching labels, such as *Latino, Asian, black, white, or multiracial*, we are often left with more questions than answers. Within the Latino category, for example, we may find individual students from the Caribbean and Central, South, and North America. We can break that down into specific countries and, still further, into categories based on distinctions in geographic region, socioeconomic class, languages spoken, or various combinations of all of these categories—the list can go on and on. The point here is that we need to look closely at who our students are without relying on overly simplistic labels. Paying close attention to differences can show that a class that looks culturally and linguistically homogeneous from the outside is actually heterogeneous and multicultural. In that vein, a Spanish bilingual teacher from Puerto Rico explains her experiences with different groups of Latino students:

> Puerto Ricans, when they come here, since they are citizens, their lives are very different and are viewed differently than a Mexican immigrant. For those kids who are born here, it's very important for them to make sure that people know that they are Americans, they feel proud. But it doesn't mean they are discarding their own culture. It's just that because they came from a different kind of situation than we did as immigrants, for them it's important.
>
> It's different for Mexican students. I used to hear teachers saying, "Oh, look he's denying his culture." The kids are saying that they're not Mexican. I said you don't understand, their parents have gone through so much being illegal here that being born here is more than just an identity thing. It's a matter of being able to be out, and not hiding, and feeling good. And yet more than us they seem to keep the culture alive even more, they keep the language more, they keep the traditions stronger. If I ask a child where they came from they say I was born here. So I think when you do multicultural education you have to look at all those issues.

Even the "American" label can have different meanings for different groups. As bilingual teachers, we can ask students to reflect and write about what it means for them to be American, Mexican, Chinese, or any other ethnicity they may bring with them.

TRY THIS!

Upper Elementary Level

Early on in the school year, have students create a social map that lists all the ways they identify and why. The important part of this activity is to offer choices while allowing complete freedom for students to include or leave out any area to which they do not feel connected. They can list family roles such as son or sister; ethnic labels such as *Latino, Chicano, Korean,* and *American;* their linguistic abilities as bi- or trilingual individuals; along with roles they play, such as student, reader, or dancer. Allow students creativity in how they design their "Who am I" social diagrams.

This activity allows students to label themselves early on, instead of succumbing to external labels they may not necessarily identify with. Display these diagrams so students can learn more about one another and learn about differences and similarities within their classroom.

HELPING STUDENTS LEARN AND LIVE WITHIN THE NEW CULTURE

While it is critical that we consider our students' home culture, we need to remember that many students in the bilingual classroom are also learning a new culture—new ways of interacting, speaking, and behaving. Sometimes, we may assume that just by living or studying within a new culture, students will automatically "get it." Although this may be the case at times, it should not be an overarching assumption. Delpit (1995) discusses the importance of the *culture of power,* which she defines as "codes or rules for participating in power" (p. 25). In the United States, such codes refer to white, middle-class cultural norms. Examples of valued essential traits range from assertiveness, to independence, to punctuality, to the use of standard or academic English. Because these codes are required for success in school and beyond, it is important that students understand what society accepts and rejects. Thus, explicitly teaching the culture of power arms students with the dominant cultural knowledge that they will need in the future—where they may be judged for either having or lacking such attributes.

Many students in bilingual classrooms do not come to school with what Bourdieu (1991) calls *cultural capital,* both the cultural and the linguistic knowledge that schools falsely presume students bring and, so, rarely teach explicitly. These areas include English language proficiency, basic literacy and numeracy skills, exposure to mainstream literature such as fairy tales, experience with museums, and even traveling abroad. Students from middle- and upper-class homes receive such exposure and are rewarded for it, while those from non-English speaking, immigrant, and low-income homes are often penalized for this lack of cultural capital. Although the latter students come to school with other languages, rich crosscultural experiences, and stories and songs about their ancestors, many teachers overlook these assets rather than interrupting the cycle.

Beyond simply teaching the culture of power, Delpit (1995) also calls for a questioning of the status quo. Students should be encouraged to consider who created these norms and why. They can also be challenged to think about how the culture of power might change if the majority group also changed.

Similarly, students can reflect on the value of bilingual skills. By conducting comparisons across languages or dialects, they will come to recognize that their medium of communication is not inferior, just different—and also useful. Michelle, a first-grade Spanish bilingual teacher in a transitional class, noticed her students' resistance to speaking their first language with her. Their preference for English and only English led her to question them about their bilingualism. She asked them to think about what a day would be like if they didn't speak or understand a word of Spanish and were unable to communicate with family members or read Spanish media and environmental print in their communities. Soon students realized the importance of an ability to speak in two languages.

In many countries, including our own, memorization and repetition of information often play a central part in instruction. As a result, some students and parents may not believe that asking questions, working in partnerships or groups, and providing critical feedback are important aspects of teaching and learning. This leaves teachers facing the dilemma of whether to accept such cultural beliefs and teach accordingly, or whether to respect those beliefs while pushing students and parents to break out of their cultural comfort zone. Since America's dominant culture purports to value democratic principles that encourage individuals to question and challenge, it becomes the role of the teacher to carefully ease students, through scaffolding and explicit explanation, into going beyond the rote memorization of facts.

Xi, a Chinese bilingual teacher from Vietnam, explains the clashes that newly arrived parents tend to experience with certain aspects of the U.S. educational system. Thanks to her Chinese proficiency, parents are able to communicate their concerns directly to her and she is able to address them:

> Some parents who are new to the country, when they come for the parent-teacher conferences, the first thing they ask me is "Where is my son's seat?" And when I show them they say, "No, I don't like that." They say, "Can you put my son in the front and not in the back?" And I tell them there's no blackboard. We don't do anything over there and when we have a mini-lesson we group them together in the meeting area, or when I have a conference, I sit with four to six students together, so basically you don't need to worry. But the point is that they don't feel comfortable. Sometimes if I complain that their child is talking too much with their friends, the parents say, "Well put them away, don't put them into a group." But right now the education is different, they need to talk, they need to participate, and so when they talk they need to face each other.

Regardless of what aspect of the dominant culture you are teaching about, one of the most effective ways to create understanding is through comparisons to students' home cultures. This allows for connections to form and helps students to see that they bring with them at least one way of knowing. Now they are adding to what they already know, becoming bicultural or multicultural.

TRY THIS!

Elementary and Secondary Level

When you meet with newly arrived parents early on in the school year, make an effort to explicitly explain the differences between schooling in the United States and in the students' home countries. To prepare for the discussion, have students make brochures or design informative posters to hang around the classroom for parents (in their native language)

(Continued)

(Continued)

that highlight key areas of difference across settings. Some areas to address might include the following:

- Classroom setup
- Learning through interaction
- Languages of instruction
- Homework

This will allow both the students and the parents to consider differences and prepare to be successful within a new context. All students can play an important role, with those who just arrived recounting their experiences abroad and those who were born or have lived in the United States explaining how different procedures and instructional practices work.

BICULTURAL IDENTITY AND STUDENT LEARNING

As a bilingual teacher, you are in a position to influence your students' identity construction process as well as their academic and linguistic growth. According to Diller and Moule (2005), "identity refers to the stable inner sense of who a person is, which is formed by the successful integration of various experiences of the self into a coherent self-image. . . . *Ethnic* identity refers to that part of personal identity that contributes to the *person's* self-image as an ethnic-group member" (p. 120). Many theorists believe that issues of children's identity are directly related to the development of ethnic attitudes, which are usually formed by the fourth grade (Katz, 1982). Recent studies have found positive associations between ethnic identity and self-esteem in minority youth.

When issues of language and culture intersect, a solid foundation in both the minority and majority languages may positively affect a sense of self. Cavallaro (2005) finds that language is central to the maintenance of ethnic heritage and identity at both the individual and group levels. Language is the carrier of culture; thus, losing one's language is equivalent to living outside of one's culture. This holds true not only for members of linguistic minority groups who speak English as a second language, but also for members of linguistic minority groups for whom English is a first language or who are at various stages of bilingual proficiency.

Anzaldúa (2004) captures the intersection of languages and cultures poetically when she writes, " if you want to really hurt me, talk badly about my language. Ethnic identity is twin skin to linguistic identity—I am my language" (p. 271). The reverse may also be true: if we want to affirm our students, we need to affirm their linguistic heritage. Lorena, a young adult of Central American heritage and a graduate of a two-way bilingual immersion program, reflects on her feelings related to the maintenance of her bilingual and bicultural heritage within her former elementary school:

> [I feel] proud, privileged because the community is so diverse but the majority is Spanish and these days you have to be able to speak Spanish and English because you are always going to find yourself in some sort of situation in which you are going to have to know either one. And there are so many more people here that speak Spanish than English [in the community], so you kind of have to know it. [It makes me feel lucky] to already be fluent and not have to learn it now because it is better to learn it when you are younger.

As children learn to value and "selectively maintain and use both cultural systems including the use of two languages in a contextually appropriate manner" (McLaughlin, 1985, p. 193), they become bicultural. Biculturalism is, as Lorena's educational experience suggests, a major goal in two-way bilingual immersion programs. The extent to which a person actively alternates between cultures determines the ease with which competency in both cultures will be maintained. People who have a flexible identity should experience less stress, whereas people who have a rigid identity often experience more. Within the bilingual classroom, students have frequent opportunities for this type of cultural switching. Reading books and authors that affirm their native culture can play a crucial part in ethnic identity formation.

There is more to identity construction, however, than the development of ethnic identity. Hawkins (2005) notes the value for children in constructing identities as learners within schools. McKay and Wong (1996) suggest that identity construction may be the mediating factor in differing levels of student academic achievement and second language learning. In other words, the development of a positive ethnic identity and academic identity appear to be linked. When students experience both social and academic success within a bilingual/bicultural environment, positive attitudes towards bilingualism/biculturalism have a firm foundation from which to grow. Such a foundation, in turn, may provide the basis for healthy identity construction.

INCORPORATING CULTURALLY RESPONSIVE PEDAGOGY IN THE CLASSROOM

The premise of *culturally responsive pedagogy* is that while we can expect all children to get to the same place eventually, the way to get there may be different for different students. These variations are rooted in students' cultural and linguistic backgrounds. Gay (2000) defines this approach as "using cultural knowledge, prior experiences, frames of reference, and performing styles of ethnically diverse students to make learning encounters more relevant and effective for them. It teaches to and through the strengths of these students" (p. 29). This means that students' cultures become an integral part of instruction, rather than merely being added on to the curriculum—for example, by focusing on a particular group during a prescribed month, such as African American History Month or Asian Heritage Month, or by celebrating representative heroes such as Martin Luther King Jr. and Rosa Parks. Such activities often take up a great deal of time and require planning that interferes with the required curriculum. They also leave many educators frustrated with all the demands placed upon them and feeling that there's just no time to teach multiculturally. But when we incorporate students' cultural backgrounds as a regular part of the curriculum, time pressures ease and instruction becomes more meaningful.

What follows is an example of how one can teach math through a culturally responsive framework. We selected this subject because it is often considered "a-cultural." In fact, when we consider how students learn various mathematical concepts and how math is used in daily life— for example, in telling time—culture is inescapable.

Gerard, a sixth-grade Haitian Creole bilingual teacher, explains how his method of solving division problems differs from that of his newly arrived students:

> Here [in the United States] you have the divisor and then the dividend; in Haiti it's the opposite. So the students, the new ones, they're like "I don't understand what you just did." So I am banging my head, how can I explain this? I had to actually relearn it because I let a couple of students do it for me so I could actually see, understand what's the confusion. My mind was reprogrammed to do division this way. . . . Even subtraction was done differently. . . . I try to show the similarities and the differences. What has been switched, what has been changed or reversed and then they say, "Oh, OK, I understand."

In this situation, the teacher had two options: to dismiss the students' method of solving division problems by only legitimizing the standard U.S. method, or to learn and incorporate the Haitian method, while comparing and contrasting the two methods against each other. By choosing the latter option and taking on the role of the learner, Gerard demonstrated a respect for the students' knowledge and culture. He also chose to build upon their math repertoire, rather than replace or locate one method as superior to another.

TRY THIS!

Upper Elementary and Secondary Level

When immigrants offer to help their children, particularly in math, they are met with, "But Mom, that's not how my teacher does it!" Approaches that do not align with the teacher or the text are automatically viewed as inferior or just plain wrong. Instead, encourage students to ask their family members, especially those who were educated in another country, how they learned to do a specific type of math problem. Ask them to document each approach, and then see how many different ways they can find to solve a given problem. Consider where the approaches came from and the pros and cons of each. If a student comes from a family with limited formal education, look for others to approach, perhaps a neighbor, older sibling, or an adult immigrant in the school.

This type of activity allows students to value the knowledge of their family and culture, while also learning that there are multiple approaches to problem solving—many that textbook authors did not even consider!

MOVING FROM A BICULTURAL TO A MULTICULTURAL CURRICULUM

My partner was reading the class a biography of Martin Luther King. So while she's teaching, an African American substitute comes to give her her prep. All the kids turned around [looked at him] and said, "Martin Luther King!" She said . . . they didn't do it on purpose, but from lack of exposure. But the fact that they saw the skin color and right away that connection . . . I think it's maybe from the kids' part, it's lack of exposure and maybe we're not reaching out to do any more cultures.

—First Grade Spanish Bilingual Teacher

Even though *Brown v. Board of Education* was decided over fifty years ago in an attempt to integrate schools, in most large cities you still find segregation along racial, cultural, linguistic, and economic lines. As a matter of fact, some cities across the United States are even more segregated now than fifty years ago (Kozol, 2005). This means that most students will attend schools with peers who come from backgrounds similar to their own and, as a result, will have limited contact with students who are culturally, racially, and economically different from themselves. Thus, learning about other cultures becomes even more important as we prepare students to participate in an interconnected and global world.

As a result of school and community segregation, most students, regardless of background, come to school with misinformation and stereotypes about different groups. Because of limited experiences with others, students often learn about the outside world from what Carlos Cortés (2000) calls the *media curriculum*. Mass media outlets play a prominent role in teaching children about others, and images about specific groups are more often used to reinforce stereotypes than to break them. Even in young children, stereotypes and prejudices become ingrained to the degree that contrary experiences and information are ignored so as not to interfere with preexisting beliefs. Research has found that "changing your opinion or belief in the face of contradictory information is one of the least likely cognitive maneuvers to be employed" (Sue, 2003, p. 28).

For teachers and students, this behavior means that exposure to the occasional story about a character that counters a stereotypical image is not enough. The vignette about Martin Luther King Jr. (MLK) illustrates how the students' relating to the black teacher as MLK could stem from their minimal exposure in the curriculum to black individuals. In other words, if MLK were the only black man they had learned about or read about in school, it would be understandable that they might only connect that name with a skin color. But if the students had read more biographies about African American men (and women) and seen depictions of African American characters in storybooks, it is likely that their reaction to this teacher would have been different. This speaks to the necessity of including consistent and frequent experiences with history, as well as images and stories that defy our notions, in order to expand our beliefs or to crush unfounded stereotypes and prejudices.

TRY THIS!

Upper Elementary and Secondary Level

Naturally, in trying to undo the stereotypical images in the media, we might want to avoid bringing popular culture into the classroom, yet a critical approach to the culture can be powerful. Ask students to search various media for representations of different cultural groups in beauty, sports, crime, health, and so on. Have them bring in sources in English and the other language. Then, conduct an analysis on how each of these groups is represented or not:

- Racial and ethnic groups
- Men and women
- Social classes
- People of different sexual orientations, religions, and abilities (when visible)

Discuss whether the media representations are fair and true or whether certain groups are singled out in ways that reinforce stereotypes. As a follow-up, students can create their own images or counter-narratives related to the topic that directly contradict prevalent stereotypes.

Teaching from a multicultural perspective is not easy. It requires that we learn about our students and incorporate their backgrounds, languages, cultures, and learning styles into instruction in meaningful ways. However, if we want students to value and understand their own backgrounds, and those of others, we cannot deny them this type of education.

TEACHING FROM A VARIETY OF PERSPECTIVES

To teach from a multicultural perspective, you should keep a few things in mind as you design curriculum and select resources. First, think about inclusion—specifically, which groups are present and which are left out? Are your students' ethnic backgrounds represented? What about those within the surrounding communities and beyond? Although considering cultural groups by ethnicity is important, we can also look at specific subcultures to include, such as those based on religion, gender, sexuality, and race.

Second, we should think about perspectives. This means that simply including a group is not enough. Learning about its point(s) of view is also critical. For example, Cristian, a Spanish fourth- and fifth-grade dual language teacher, assigned his students to examine how Native Americans are represented across popular media outlets. He first had the class watch mainstream movies like *Peter Pan* to consider the perspective of Native Americans, how they are viewed, and who created the movie. The students examined how Native Americans were portrayed in print media and in a nonfiction National Geographic recording on Native Americans. Then they compared the viewpoints of the three. While it is nearly impossible to present all perspectives (you could probably spend all year on one topic if that was your intent), introducing students to a variety of cultures helps them understand that there is more than one way of knowing.

The third point to consider is voice, which takes inclusion and perspective a step further. By considering who gets to tell the story, we allow students to see which voices are present and which are suppressed. This does not mean that *outsider voices* are not valued, but it reinforces the importance of firsthand experiences. For example, reading about Korean American culture only from the viewpoint of European American authors may lead to an inauthentic and unbalanced account.

While this is a lot to consider, it is important if we want students to have a holistic education—especially in the absence of direct interaction with other cultural groups. By starting from students' own cultural backgrounds, learning about the new culture, and then branching outward, we can enable children and youth to develop the strong self-concept and cross-cultural understandings that are required to thrive in our multicultural world.

MULTICULTURAL THEORETICAL CONNECTIONS

Each of the multicultural theories we have discussed focuses on a different aspect of student difference, yet there is consistency between them. These approaches position students first to value their own backgrounds and then to acquire knowledge that can be turned into cultural capital and used to critique, question, and challenge the culture of power. This is an additive approach to culture that parallels an additive approach to language. It is also a transformative approach and the subject of chapter three.

Return to the Essential Question

Why does culture matter so much in the bilingual classroom?

One Teacher's Response

I [Tatyana] came to the United States at the age of six, from the former Soviet Union. Not speaking a word of English other than "yes" and "no," I quickly understood the importance of speaking English, and only English. I rapidly abandoned the Russian language, to the extent that if my parents spoke Russian to me in public I would cringe in embarrassment. I was easily able to "cover up" any differences that could hint at my immigrant background. Unlike my parents, I had no identifiable "foreign" accent, I insisted that everyone call me Tanya, which to me sounded more "American" than Tatyana, and I never spoke of being born in a different country or speaking a different language. It was my secret . . . until sixth grade. That year my teacher, Ms. Chang, invited my mother to the class to speak about our immigration experience as well as the anti-Semitism that forced us to leave our home country. Initial feelings of reluctance and embarrassment of having my mother speak to my peers (in sixth grade no less!) about a topic I never mentioned and went to great lengths to conceal quickly subsided and shifted to surprise and pride. Surprise because of the interest my classmates took in learning about our family history and pride that I was different, in a good way. (Thank you Ms. Chang!)

All teachers can and must find ways to show students that their languages and cultures are not just valuable tools for learners, but valuable parts of who they are. Ms. Chang realized that by making her students' backgrounds a central part of the curriculum, she at the same time validated their experiences as she exposed the rest of the class to a topic that, until that day, only existed in the pages of their social studies textbook. While making content culturally relevant takes more time and effort, it will undoubtedly lead to increased interest, connections, and learning for students. In the next chapter, we will take a deeper, more focused look at ways to make learning meaningful for emergent bilingual students.

REFERENCES

Anzaldúa, G. (2004). Linguistic terrorism. In O. Santa Ana (Ed.), *Tongue-tied: The lives of multilingual children in public education*. New York: Rowman and Littlefield.

Asante, M. K. (1991). *The Afrocentric idea in education*. Philadelphia: Temple University Press.

Bourdieu, P. (1991). *Language and symbolic power.* Cambridge, MA: Harvard University Press.

Cavallaro, F. (2005). Language maintenance revisited: An Australian perspective. *Bilingual Research Journal, 29*(3), 561–582.

Cortés, C. E. (2000). *The children are watching: How the media teach about diversity.* New York: Teachers College Press.

Delpit, L. (1995). *Other people's children: Culture conflict in the classroom.* New York: New Press.

Diller, J. V., & Moule, J. (2005). *Cultural competence: A primer for educators.* Belmont, CA: Thomson Wadsworth.

Gay, G. (2000). *Culturally responsive teaching: Theory, research, and practice.* New York: Teachers College Press.

Hawkins, M. R. (2005). Becoming a student: Identity work and academic literacies in early schooling. *TESOL Quarterly, 39*(1), 59–81.

Katz, P. A. (1982). *Development of children's racial awareness and intergroup attitudes.* (Report No. PS 012 321). Norwood, NJ: Ablex Publishing Corporation. (ERIC Document Reproduction Services No. ED 207 675).

Kozol, J. (2005). *The shame of the nation: The restoration of apartheid schooling in America.* New York: Crown.

McKay, S. L., & Wong, S. L. C. (1996). Multiple discourse, multiple identities: Investment and agency in second-language learning among Chinese adolescent immigrant students. *Harvard Educational Review, 66*(3), 577–608.

McLaughlin, B. (1985). *Second language acquisition in childhood (Vol. 2): School-age children.* Hillsdale, NJ: Erlbaum.

Nieto, S. (2002). *Language, culture, and teaching: Critical perspectives for a new century.* Mahwah, NJ: Erlbaum.

Reyes, S. A., & Vallone, T .L. (2008). *Constructivist strategies for teaching English language learners.* Thousand Oaks, CA: Corwin.

Sue, D. W. (2003). *Overcoming our racism: The journey to liberation.* San Francisco: Jossey-Bass.

3

Curriculum and Instruction

Essential Question

Is teaching in a minority language really any different from teaching in English in a mainstream classroom?

One Teacher's Dilemma

The coordinator of our district's K–12 Russian language program has made it a point to remind me of the countless hours that have been spent adapting books for our program. With picture books, this has meant covering up the English text with Russian text in a durable format that little fingers cannot easily destroy. Of course, everything must be perfectly translated and edited—a tremendously time-consuming task. With academic texts and trade books, that means an extensive process of translation. We cannot do those ourselves, so we obtain permission from the publisher to translate and send them out to be professionally done—again, at tremendous cost.

Recently, more options have become available for purchasing texts in the original Russian language. But our students are from an "Old Believer" background; they are from a group of religious dissenters who split from the dominant Russian Orthodox Church in the mid-1600s and have forged separate customs and traditions, so there may be a cultural gap we need to consider. Books from modern-day Russia may pose some cultural discrepancies for these students. While we are fortunate to have a K–12 Russian program, it also poses cultural and linguistic challenges when it comes to books and other educational materials.

Bilingual teachers must continuously consider language learning and culture—and the subsequent impact on classroom curriculum and instruction. In addition, as the preceding educator noted, while instructional materials in languages other than English are becoming easier to obtain, choices are not as limitless as they are for those in the English language. Furthermore, few options exist in languages such as Mandarin, Vietnamese, Russian, and Korean. Literature and instructional materials in languages without a long-standing written tradition, such as Yup'ik or Navaho, have only recently become available, as orthographies have been created and perfected. When there is a discrepancy between the language of instruction and the availability of instructional materials, educators are left to fill the gap. When no guidance is provided on how to adapt instructional materials meant for a monolingual context to a bilingual context, educators are left to fill this gap as well.

TRY THIS!

Elementary Level

Decide which picture books you would like your bilingual students to have access to in their L1 literacy development. If they are not available in the native language of your students, translate the text and cover the English text with the translation. Make certain to cover the new text with a laminate for durability. Although this involves translation, it is the educator, not the student, who is doing the translation. If your school is able and willing to invest funds in this project, seek assistance from others who are appropriately prepared to do such translations. Have teaching assistants apply the laminate covers.

TEACHING METHODS AND STRATEGIES ARE NOT UNIVERSAL

Sometimes, they don't understand why we give more abstract homework; they want them to do specific pages from a book and problems. Also, they are used to very structured, traditional classrooms, but we do more group work.

Beth, a Russian bilingual teacher, makes it abundantly clear that teaching methods are not universal. In fact, a comparison of past and current popular educational methodologies reveals that, even within the same country or general culture, methodologies change and develop. It is thus crucial to examine the methodologies highlighted in your students' countries of origin before planning instruction. You will need to consider which method(s) you will use and whether you will need to make the bridge from one method to another.

TRY THIS!

Elementary and Secondary Level

Collaborate with knowledgeable adults (educators, parents, community members, or older students) from the target culture to learn about the dominant content and literacy methodologies and strategies used in that culture. Help students bridge the difference by explicitly contrasting both methods. Help them create strategies that work with the new methodologies by modeling your thinking process out loud. Ask your students to do the same for other classmates.

Scarcity of curricular materials and adapting teaching methodologies to student needs are only two of the several challenges that bilingual teachers must address. Clearly, if the answer to this chapter's essential question, "Is teaching in a minority language really any different from teaching in English in a mainstream classroom?" was a simple "no," there would not be a need for this book. What, then, is the difference? We suggest that, in addition to locating or creating appropriate instructional materials, considering teaching methodologies prevalent in the country of origin, and addressing the linguistic and cultural considerations discussed in Chapters 1 and 2, something deeper is necessitated. Providing a quality education to language-minority students demands moving away from a traditional transmission model of education and moving toward a constructivist stance. In order to understand what this entails, it is first necessary to understand exactly what is meant by the words *educational philosophy, methodology,* and *strategy* and to examine how they are separate but interrelated concepts.

EDUCATIONAL PHILOSOPHY, METHODOLOGY, AND STRATEGIES

We all hold an educational philosophy, just as we all hold life philosophies, whether we are consciously aware of it or not. If we think that we do not hold a philosophy, chances are that we are buying into a mainstream philosophy, which is the norm. Often, we are not consciously aware of our educational or life philosophy unless it comes into conflict with what is commonly accepted in society. For example, the transmission model of education, an approach in which teachers and texts serve as suppliers of knowledge while students act as empty receptacles waiting to be filled, is widely used in U.S. schools. Formalized tests are then used to measure the success of this knowledge-transmission process. Our thinking about educational philosophy tends to develop further if we challenge this conventional thinking about pedagogy. Questioning the transmission model pushes us to ask whether or not students should be in a passive relationship to the teacher and to each other. Of course, it is the responsibility of the teacher-education institution to provide a background in educational philosophy for preservice and continuing teachers. Some colleges and universities do a better job at this than others. However, even when a solid foundation is provided, educators should always be aware of the ever-changing landscape of knowledge and thought on educational philosophy.

Using a textbook as the main curricular source for classroom content would be acceptable within a transmission approach but unacceptable within either a constructivist or a critical approach (see pages 48–49). In a constructivist or critical approach, curriculum cannot be so narrowly defined. Rather, it is viewed as the entire organized environment for teaching and learning within a classroom or classroom community. Schubert (1986) discusses curriculum more broadly in terms of that which is worthwhile to know and experience. He also believes the *hidden curriculum* (what is taught implicitly rather than explicitly) and the *null curriculum* (what is taught by not being taught) hold equal weight with that which is explicitly taught. Having students answer questions from a text, with the teacher deciding on the correctness of the response, is acceptable pedagogy emanating from a transmission approach to education. Again, however, it is incompatible with a constructivist or critical approach. In such classrooms, pedagogy is interactive, the student perspective is valued, and there is less distinction between "right" and "wrong" answers.

Just as curriculum and pedagogy flow from educational philosophy, methodology flows from curriculum and pedagogy. "Methods are used by teachers to create learning environments and to specify the nature of the activity in which the teacher and learner will be involved during the lesson" (Saskatchewan Education, 1991, p. 3). Examples of methodology include writing workshops, scientific inquiry, cooperative learning, experiential learning, and project-based learning. Strategies, in turn, flow from methodology and represent the specific activities in which the learners will be engaged. Examples of strategies include brainstorming, writing in journals, taking field notes, conducting experiments, small and large group discussions, answering questions, modeling, demonstrations, problem solving, partner reading, and jigsawing. Although particular strategies are often associated with particular methodologies (for example, jigsawing is often used with cooperative grouping), many methodologies employ a wide variety of strategies. Project-based learning, for example, could use virtually all of the strategies named above. The relationship between educational philosophy, methodology, and strategies is illustrated in Figures 3.1, 3.2, and 3.3.

For systemic change to occur in a manner that maximizes benefits for ELLs, it is essential to first examine the educational philosophy underlying the school or school system. As philosophy drives program model, which in turn drives curriculum and instruction, which in turn

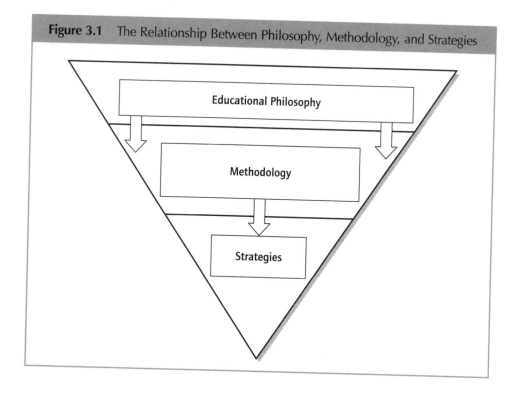

Figure 3.1 The Relationship Between Philosophy, Methodology, and Strategies

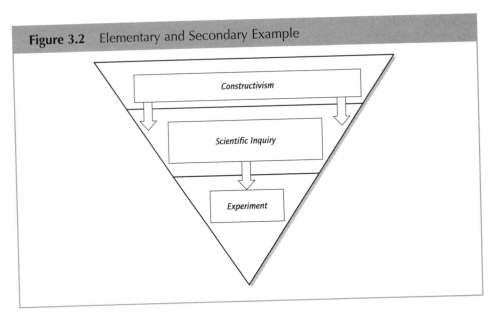

Figure 3.2 Elementary and Secondary Example

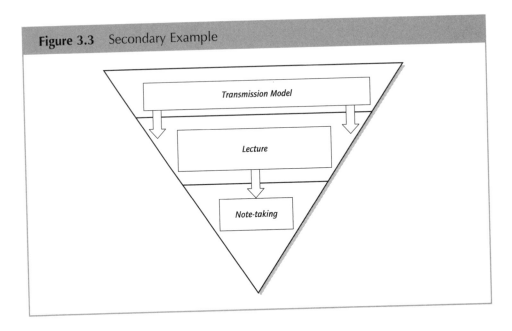

Figure 3.3 Secondary Example

drives instructional practice (through methodology and strategies), what is happening in a given classroom may not necessarily be entirely up to the teacher.

In an exemplary school, there should be a seamless transition from educational philosophy to program model to curriculum and pedagogy to instructional practice. For example, in a classroom within a school that has adopted a constructivist approach, the curriculum might, in part, be considered the outside world (such as a local animal habitat). The teacher might use project-based methodology to study the natural ecosystem, acting as facilitator of the learning environment. The teacher might use strategies such as taking field notes and problem posing. Understanding ecological problems caused by humankind through this interactive experience would be consistent with a constructivist approach. Taking action to help save endangered animal habitats would flow from a critical approach. In other words, it is the stance (philosophical approach) that we take as educators that dictates the curriculum we highlight and the teaching practices in which we engage.

When educators, from administrators to teachers, do not understand this instructional flow, the result is often a disjointed education. Expecting students to formulate and ask their own questions one year and then merely answer literal questions from a text the next year is not an optimal educational situation. If the rules in our own households changed from year to year, week to week, or day to day, we would find it difficult to function. In general, they do not—because our rules and routines tend to be based upon our own life philosophies. Schools should be no different.

TRY THIS!

Elementary and Secondary Level

Look at Figure 3.1, which outlines the flow from teaching philosophy to methodology to strategy. Think of an area or concept that is traditionally taught through a transmission approach. Consider how the chart would look if you started from a constructivist philosophy. Fill out the methodology and strategy section of the chart and take a risk in teaching the concept using a different approach. Then reflect on how student learning was impacted.

IMPACT OF EDUCATIONAL PHILOSOPHY, METHODOLOGY, AND STRATEGIES ON BILINGUAL PROGRAMS

Educational philosophy determines program models in contexts that serve emergent bilingual students. Districts and schools that have a good grasp of language acquisition and language-learning theory will support additive program models of bilingual instruction, which allow for the acquisition of a second language while maintaining and developing the first, if resources allow. The model chosen will in turn impact curriculum and pedagogy. For example, two-way bilingual immersion models mandate a strict separation of the L1 and the L2, and the integration of language and content learning are central to their success. Obviously, this has profound implications for both curriculum and pedagogy because teachers will choose instructional methodologies and strategies that follow this agenda (e.g., the integration of language and content and natural language acquisition processes).

We can see the importance, then, of having as a base for exemplary bilingual educational practice a program model that can support ELLs academically, linguistically, and socially. Such a model must be based on a philosophy that values the native language and culture of the student, in addition to valuing the process of acquiring the L2 language and culture. In other words, such a model must stress culturally responsive pedagogy, an approach to teaching that draws upon students' identities and backgrounds as central to the formation of meaning in the educational process, thus validating prior knowledge and cultural heritage. Notice that students' identities and backgrounds are highlighted in this approach, forcing a discussion not only of academic, linguistic, and social skills, but of identity construction as well.

As we can see, bilingual educators are informed by more than linguistic and cultural concerns. We must go to the heart of curriculum and instruction to make certain that our approach, methodologies, and strategies will support our students. We suggest that both a constructivist and a critical philosophy will drive the appropriate curriculum for ELLs. In Chapter 6, however, we will discuss how modifications must also be made for ELLs to accommodate linguistic and cultural differences.

CREATING AN L1 CONSTRUCTIVIST CLASSROOM FOR EMERGENT BILINGUAL STUDENTS

Reyes and Vallone (2008, pp. 36–37) note the following principles that guide a constructivist educational philosophy:

- New learning builds on prior knowledge
- Learning is mediated through social interaction

- Problem solving is part of learning
- Learning is a process, and teachers are facilitators of that process

Reyes and Vallone (2008, pp. 73–78) caution that critical pedagogy "is not a list of steps for successful instruction"; rather, it is "fluid" and "intended to be shaped by teachers and learners together." They offer the following principles to define this philosophy:

- Critical pedagogy is not prescriptive: teaching and learning emerge as students and teachers position themselves in the world.
- Critical teachers do not lecture: they are facilitators who instruct through dialogue.
- Critical pedagogy does not ignore the white elephant in the room: it names social problems and develops critical consciousness.
- Critical pedagogy does not maintain the status quo: it is essentially transformative.

TRY THIS!

Upper Elementary and Secondary Levels

If you are a critical educator and are required by your school or district to make a standard textbook the starting point for your instruction, use this as an opportunity to engage your students in critique. For example, if you are using a history text with a unit on the Vietnam War, try the following activities:

- Invite Vietnam veterans to your classroom to talk about their experiences and perspectives
- Invite speakers to your classroom who can talk about their prior activism as Vietnam War protestors
- Invite family members to your classroom who can speak about how they experienced the Vietnam war through the media and through their own lived experiences
- Bring in alternate sources of information that express views other than those found in the text
- Bring in primary documents about the Vietnam War
- Watch significant parts of documentaries, movies, and news clips that provide varied perspectives on the Vietnam War

(Continued)

(Continued)

Note discrepancies in the various sources of information. Encourage the students to pose problems through both writing and discussion. Engage the students in an analysis of your history text in particular and of mandated educational texts in general. Have different students write essays about the Vietnam War from different perspectives. Share these essays with the class. Produce a classroom-made book on the Vietnam War as seen from multiple perspectives.

Remember, these activities can be done in either the L1 or the L2, or both. Some of the speakers and documents could be in one language or the other. Likewise, the final classroom-made book could be in either the L1 or the L2, or it could be bilingual. Consistency is the key in language use here. Do not mix languages within a session unless there is a specific reason to do so.

CONSTRUCTIVIST CLASSROOMS AND CULTURALLY RESPONSIVE PEDAGOGY

Reyes and Vallone (2008) suggest that "culturally responsive pedagogy can be thought of as a type of cultural constructivism" (p. 12). Because culturally responsive pedagogy uses the students' backgrounds as a starting point in the curriculum, it quite naturally promotes native language and culture—making it compatible with both constructivist education and second-language-acquisition and learning theory. As noted previously, it may also encourage healthy identity construction and the development of positive self-esteem.

TRY THIS!

Elementary and Secondary Levels

After first demonstrating and modeling the activity, distribute large sheets of Manila paper to the students. Have students write their first name vertically in large, bold capital letters down the page. For each letter in their names, have them write a word that has something to do with their own or their family's immigrant heritage.

This exercise was adapted from Reyes and Vallone (2008). They described how one teacher (Monica) conducted an opening L2 social studies unit on immigration for an eighth-grade bilingual classroom comprised of students from an immigrant heritage. Following is how the teacher highlighted in the Reyes and Vallone narrative described herself:

```
c   o   m   M   u   n   i   t   y
            O   p   p   r   e   s   s   i   o   n
            N   e   g   l   i   g   e   n   c   e
            I   m   m   i   g   r   a   n   t
        a   C   t   i   v   i   s   t
    t   r   A   n   s   i   t   i   o   n
```

ADAPTING CURRICULUM DESIGNED FOR MONOLINGUAL CLASSROOMS

In the current climate of standardization and one-size-fits-all approaches, it's likely that your school or district has adopted a curriculum or program that all teachers must follow. While there are aspects of most curricular models that are effective, many have not been created with ELLs or bilingual programs in mind. Instead, they are designed for English-only classrooms with English-dominant speakers. In the best-case scenarios, there may be translations or accommodations for language learners available; at worst, you may be expected to create your own translations and perhaps make modifications. Since there are few curriculum models specifically made for bilingual students and programs, you will need to modify the content, language, and pedagogy to best meet the needs of your students.

Most curricular programs focus on a given content area with little emphasis on language, other than the occasional vocabulary list. As a bilingual teacher, you are always involved in simultaneous content and language instruction. Therefore, you will need to think about how you are making language accessible for your students by focusing on an aspect of language that is specific to the genre of the content area you are studying. In addition, content that is less familiar to students can be made more manageable by making explicit the connections to student backgrounds and experiences.

Most programs are grounded in a specific cultural perspective, which may not represent that of your students. This does not mean you need to disregard the program completely, but it does require additional effort on your part. First, you can view this as an opportunity to discuss one-sidedness and (limited exposure to) differing points of view. For instance, if your social studies book has a section on the Mexican-American War from the U.S. perspective, this can provide a useful opening for a discussion on whose history matters. (We suggest consideration of the saying "We didn't cross the border, the border crossed us.") Beyond these discussions, you can also look for additional sources that broaden the perspectives presented.

A common pedagogical approach to teaching literacy in schools is the *workshop model*. In general, it requires that daily reading and writing lessons include a mini-lesson focused on a given skill, practice in groups, related independent work, conferencing with the teacher, and a whole-group share. The implementation of the model can be rigid, with time limits for each section. In bilingual programs, however, teachers may need additional time to scaffold for language. Maurice, a Haitian Creole bilingual teacher, speaks about the workshop model and its one-size-fits-all format, which has both negative and positive effects on his students:

> What could apply to one group of students cannot apply to another group. When it comes to the workshop model, we have kids who can really work in groups and others that cannot. . . . There are students that need to be guided all the time. Now, as a teacher we have to do what we need to do just for the needs of these children sometimes. So the workshop model doesn't allow you the freedom to do this and that. . . . [However,] you have an opportunity to pull out some of the kids and work with specific skills. That's the positive aspect; it lets you give students individual attention, especially when it comes to conferences.

To make the workshop model work for her students, Araceli, a Spanish bilingual teacher, has to add in a "mini-mini-lesson" before the required mini-lesson by using visuals, building up her students' vocabulary, and getting them to see what experiences they have had that will help them connect with the content. Whether your school has adapted the workshop model or another one of the myriad programs available, it's likely that there are positive aspects. But in a bilingual classroom, modifications, accommodations, and supplemental resources will be necessary in order to engage and meet the academic and linguistic needs of your students.

Depending on your administration's and district's understanding of bilingual education and second language learning, you may be provided with leeway in how to implement a given curriculum or, to the contrary, you may be expected to stay in lockstep with all the teachers at your grade level. If the latter is your situation, you will be placed in the roles of both educator and advocate for your students. You may have to explain why you need to make changes in the curriculum, based on bilingual theories and research. You may also have to speak up when new models are presented that disregard the needs of bilingual students and programs. Only through voicing your concerns can those who make far-reaching decisions concerning curriculum be made aware of the different needs of and considerations for bilingual settings.

Return to the Essential Question

Is teaching in a minority language really any different from teaching in English in a mainstream classroom?

One Teacher's Response

Araceli, a Spanish bilingual teacher, explains how the curriculum and methods of teaching social studies and science go beyond simply reading about a given concept:

> And even social studies . . . you need to go out into the community. You need to do a lot of that kind of exposure. So I have a beautiful library about families and communities, but that's not it. We were integrating it through the read alouds. Science is about exploring, children have to learn how to ask questions and explore and observe, the whole process of a scientific mind.

When teachers are sensitive to the linguistic and cultural heritage of their students, they become avid observers and learners and are able to simultaneously integrate both language and culture into the classroom curriculum. This is cultural constructivism: the union of constructivist practice and culturally responsive pedagogy (Reyes & Vallone, 2008). This type of teaching, combined with a bilingual curriculum grounded in principles of second language learning, is what makes teaching in bilingual contexts unique. When teachers are also able to combine this with a critical stance, the learning environment for ELLs can be profound. Therefore, there are some principle areas where teaching in a bilingual classroom is similar to teaching in a mainstream setting. For instance, both require the same careful attention to teaching philosophies that allow students to co-create knowledge and develop their understandings while putting related methods and strategies in place. However, teaching in a linguistically diverse classroom requires paying additional attention to students' backgrounds, because the integration of their cultures and language learning needs are central to the teaching and learning process. It also requires that additional attention be focused on teaching bilingually across the content areas, as will be explored in the subsequent chapter.

REFERENCES

Nieto, S. (2004). *Affirming diversity: The sociopolitical context of multicultural education.* New York: Pearson Education.

Reyes, S. A., & Vallone, T. L. (2008). *Constructivist strategies for teaching English language learners.* Thousand Oaks, CA: Corwin.

Saskatchewan Education. (1991). *Instructional approaches: A framework for professional practice.* Regina, Saskatchewan, Canada: Saskatchewan Education.

Schubert, W. H. (1986). *Curriculum: Perspective, paradigm, and possibility.* New York: Macmillan.

4

Teaching Bilingually Across the Content Areas

By contributing author Irma M. Olmedo

Essential Question

What approaches should teachers consider for teaching content to English language learners in bilingual classrooms?

Two Teachers' Dilemmas

Ms. Parker was perplexed about the challenge she was having teaching the curriculum to her fourth-grade students. "I hear the kids speaking English in the playground and in the lunchroom and they seem to have no problem communicating. But when we start working with our content area curriculum, they seem lost. Why is it that they can talk in English with their classmates but I get blank stares when we start discussing what I'm trying to teach them in the classroom?"

Ms. Torres, who was fluent in Spanish, voiced similar concerns. "I'm able to teach them in Spanish, but I find that it's still challenging having them understand all that's going on. Just because I teach them in Spanish doesn't mean that they always get it. They even have trouble reading some of the Spanish books."

A s illustrated in the above vignettes, the language of instruction alone does not determine what makes for effective instruction for ELLs. As will be seen in this chapter, other considerations must be taken into account to effectively teach ELLs in the bilingual classroom.

GRADE LEVEL CONTENT IN MATH, SCIENCE, AND SOCIAL STUDIES

There are several important issues that bilingual teachers or those teaching ELLs need to consider, regardless of the language of instruction. First of all, teachers must remember that children need to move from *learning to read* to *reading to learn*. Reading skills will be used to broaden knowledge of areas such as mathematics, science, and social studies. It is this critical step that decides whether children are able to keep up with the mainstream curriculum that is taught to their peers.

One of the most important reasons for teaching ELLs in a bilingual classroom is to ensure that the content areas of the curriculum are made accessible to them. The bilingual teacher must move beyond teaching only survival English to teaching academic language so that children can communicate. She or he needs to teach the curriculum to students so that they can learn what all students are expected to learn at each grade level. This is especially critical if these teachers are involved in transitional bilingual programs that move students into the mainstream classroom in three years or less—at which time they will be exposed to instruction only in English and be expected to keep up with their English-speaking peers. The bilingual students will not be successful in those classrooms unless they were exposed to the curricular content that was being covered in the mainstream English-language classroom while they were learning English.

It is important for teachers to recognize that non-English speaking students can learn the content of the curriculum and the related concepts. The fact that children do not know English should not deny them access to the same challenging and rich curriculum that is provided to mainstream students. Moreover, if teachers are concerned about equity and opening up opportunities to their bilingual students, they must teach not only English but also all the areas of the curriculum in a way that allows students to access that content. Students should not be expected to wait until they have attained a certain level of English to learn math, science, and social studies.

This is why instruction in the native language is so critical for these students. It can make a significant difference in helping them develop concepts and content knowledge in the standard curriculum (Cummins, 1991). If children are placed in classrooms with a teacher who can teach in their non-English native language, they can continue to make academic progress while learning English at a different time of the day. When teachers can develop concepts in the child's L1, the language that is spoken in the home and which they use with their peers, there is minimal need to translate or to develop the kinds of strategies that would be necessary if the instruction took place in the L2, leaving students struggling to understand even the most basic directions. Moreover, if teachers have large numbers of students who are functioning in their social language in the L1 and can be grouped together for instruction, they may also be able to avail themselves of content area materials in the L1 in order to teach the concepts. Several textbook companies have published content area materials in Spanish that parallel the English textbook series that are used in mainstream English classrooms. In those classrooms, teaching in the L1 might be the approach that will most easily facilitate the learning of content area concepts. In addition, the development of the L1 can have many other cognitive and social benefits because this language becomes an additional tool in their skills repertoire (Olmedo, 2005).

A large proportion of the ELLs in U.S. schools are Spanish speakers. Frequently, these children are in schools where they are also in the majority and in neighborhoods where Spanish is the principal language of communication. This is another advantage in using the native language with them—it offers the least amount of challenge in the transition between home and school. The language spoken by parents in the home is the same language spoken by the teacher and students in the school. If homework were sent home, most parents would be able to help—or at least understand what it is that the children are learning. If educators believe that the educational process should be a partnership between the school and the home, then the use of the student's native language is essential for student success.

Some schools assert that they can use a sheltered English approach with students who have not mastered enough English to comprehend instruction in English mainstream classrooms. Although there is a place for sheltered English, this approach is only appropriate when students have reached the intermediate level of English proficiency. If ELLs are not exposed to curricular content in their native language before they reach this intermediate level of English, they will be unable to keep up with their peers when they transition to English-only classrooms.

CONTENT STANDARDS
AND THE DISTRICT CURRICULUM

Pedagogy for teaching in bilingual and ESL classrooms needs to be based on the goals and objectives of the curriculum and the state and district standards. These standards are generally published in state and district documents, and teachers may be expected to develop their lesson and unit plans with reference to them. Often, the state standards are broad statements that relate to the development of skills such as literacy and numeracy, whereas district standards may become more specific, in some cases identifying knowledge that students need to develop in specific content areas (such as, "students will be able to explain how a bill becomes a law"). Bilingual and ESL teachers often have a double set of standards to consult: the content area standards that apply to all students and the specific English-language proficiency standards that many states have developed to provide guidance for teachers in these classrooms. The World-Class Instructional Design and Assessment (WIDA) standards, for example, have been developed by several states as part of a consortium. They address language proficiency in both social and academic language and in all four skills of listening, speaking, reading, and writing. These standards can be a helpful guide as teachers consider when to transition students from a bilingual classroom into one in which they no longer receive instruction in their native language.

In addition to organizing instruction in reference to the standards, teachers need to recognize that all teaching should build on what the students already know. They need to gauge children's level of knowledge before starting to teach new content. Teachers cannot assume that ELLs possess the same background as students in mainstream classrooms. Given the diversity of students in ESL or bilingual classrooms, including their range of prior educational experiences, they may be lacking in some areas. On the other hand, they may be knowledgeable in areas that mainstream students are not. Moll (2005) has noted that these *funds of knowledge* should be tapped for a variety of reasons—because they may help students learn new concepts by building on what they know, because they will have a positive effect on self-concept when the teacher acknowledges that ELLs know something that others do not, and because it is important for other students to recognize that ELLs have background knowledge built from their own experiences.

The often-used KWL strategy (what do you *know*, what do you *want* to know, and what have you *learned*) is a useful tool for teachers to employ as they seek to discover their ELLs' strengths and weaknesses. In spite of its simplicity, the KWL strategy can be an excellent approach for engaging

ELLs in the kind of verbal interaction that too often gets shortchanged when teachers are focused on "teaching the basics." What can be more basic than being able to express what you know about a topic and to raise questions for which you would like to find answers? In addition, it can be a form of review and assessment at the end of a unit of instruction so that the teacher can assess not only what students have learned but also what may need to be retaught.

TEACHING MATHEMATICS

Some people mistakenly believe that mathematics is easy to teach to ELLs because its language is universal. This is not the case. Teaching mathematics is more than teaching computation skills. There is a specialized language in math that learners need to be exposed to, especially if they are to engage in solving word problems. Mathematics has specialized vocabulary and needs to be learned not only in the L1 but also in the L2 if students are to tackle the subject matter and engage in higher order thinking skills (Licon-Khisty & Viego, 1999). Furthermore, with the growing emphasis on the ability of students to explain how problems are solved, the active use of this vocabulary needs to become an important component of learning how to do math.

When teaching mathematics concepts in English or the native language, be aware of multiple ways of explaining the same operations. For example, in teaching subtraction skills, Spanish uses terms such as *quitar, restar, menos de,* and *cuál es la diferencia.* Students have to learn that all this terminology calls for the same operation. Similarly, English uses terms such as *less than, fewer than, minus, subtract from, take away,* and *difference between.* Students have to learn all the different ways of expressing the same operation if they are to solve mathematics problems correctly. This vocabulary cannot merely be memorized but must be actively used to communicate in the language of mathematics. It is not enough for students to be able to recognize the vocabulary in texts; they must be able to actively use it to explain what a problem calls for and how they arrived at a solution.

There are many hands-on materials that can be used to teach mathematics concepts, such as geoboards and Cuisenaire rods. It is important for teachers to avail themselves of such resources, which limit the need for extensive vocabulary in the initial stages of teaching a new computation or technique. This is especially valuable for ELLs who may understand the concepts and operations but may not have developed the vocabulary and grammatical structures to express their knowledge in English. Even if they are being taught in the L1, use of manipulatives enhances comprehension and visualization of the mathematical operations.

Teachers should also try to employ culturally relevant examples to teach problem solving. It need not always be the case that Mike is ordering pizza for his birthday party. It could also be that Antonio is helping his mother make tamales.

TRY THIS!

Elementary Level

Doña Lupe is getting ready for the family holiday celebration. This means a lot of cooking of tamales, one of the favorite family specialties. Antonio and Carmen always help her and even use math to make sure that they cook enough tamales for the whole family. Doña Lupe has 3 sisters; one of them has 4 children, another has 2 children, and the third one has 3. Doña Lupe wants to have at least 2 tamales for each child and 3 for each adult. Since the children's fathers are also coming to the party, how many tamales does Doña Lupe have to prepare? She also knows that one pound of masa (dough) makes 6 tamales. How many pounds does she need to prepare for all of them? (You can elaborate on this problem by asking how much money she has to spend to buy the ingredients.)

An important and exciting innovation in this area is the effort by some educators to teach mathematics for social justice (Gutstein, 2003). This approach aims not only to use culturally relevant content, as the Try This! example illustrates, but also to show children the relevance of mathematical operations for solving social problems such as unemployment, budget deficits, issues of war and peace, economic inequality, and so on. Some classroom teachers also use mathematics to help children comprehend the large numbers they will need to make sense of federal budget deficits and demographics (Gutstein & Peterson, 2005). They use a Freirian orientation that aims at "reading the word to read the world"—employing mathematics literacy to understand problems in the world around them (Freire & Macedo, 1987).

TEACHING SCIENCE

One of the critical issues in content area teaching is the movement away from transmission models of instruction and toward more inquiry-based approaches (for more detail, see Chapter 3). This is particularly important when teaching science, which by its nature aims to foster the skills of raising questions, hypothesizing, making inferences, exploring answers, and gathering data—rather than memorizing predetermined answers to questions. Children are inherently curious, and teachers should capitalize on that by considering what makes them curious and then building science inquiry projects based on such questions.

What is true for the language of mathematics is also true for the language of science: it is complex and specialized. Scientific writing takes on challenging vocabulary and grammatical structures. It is characterized by the frequent use of the passive voice, nominalizations, the embedding of grammatical elements within each other, and the use of subordinate clauses. Complex sentences take longer to process, especially for ELLs. Therefore, teaching science content entails actively teaching the language of science and providing many opportunities for students to use it. Direct instruction in such language forms is both legitimate and necessary. Scientific vocabulary should be taught directly, whether in the L1 or L2, and students should have opportunities to practice using the vocabulary to engage in inquiry.

An important value of science teaching is the opportunity to promote cooperative learning. Such partner or group work is valuable not only for the purposes of problem solving and social skills, but also for enhancing language fluency and communicative competence. Students need many opportunities to talk with adults and peers if their language development is to be enhanced. In addition, since classroom inquiry requires academic language usage, many opportunities should be provided for students to do things such as ask questions of each other, agree and disagree, defend a position, and explain how they came up with the answer. All of these discussions promote the use of a variety of language functions, whether in the L1 or the L2.

Science is also an ideal subject for organizing learning centers where students can actively manipulate materials and extend their knowledge. They can hypothesize, observe, collect data, measure, and state conclusions based on these procedures. This, in essence, is the scientific method, the core approach for teaching and learning science. Even if a teacher does not have access to a science lab, it is still possible to engage in hands-on science and to involve students in inquiry. Many scientific experiments do not require fancy or expensive instruments. Materials as simple as measuring cups, mixing bowls, scales, rulers, magnets, house plants, and magnifying glasses can help enhance skills (such as observation, measurement, hypothesizing, testing, and experimentation) that characterize the scientific method. The outdoors is often a wonderful place from which to begin the process of scientific inquiry.

TRY THIS!

Upper Elementary Level

Organize a learning center in your room with a variety of tools, such as magnifying glasses, water-droppers, small containers, microscopes with slides, and spoons, which students can use to collect data about a particular phenomenon. Conduct investigations, for example, about how life develops in water under specific conditions, such as with or without light, or with different types or rocks or soil underneath. Have students record their observations and measurements over time, discuss and compare them with partners, and reach conclusions about what different life forms need in order to grow. Provide students with observation sheets to record what they are discovering. Small groups of students can use the science learning center while other students are engaged in different activities, such as visiting the classroom library to read about related phenomena.

One resource that can be quite valuable for teachers is the local science museum, which often provides boxes and kits for inquiry-based science lessons. In Chicago, for example, the Field Museum makes such resources available to teachers, with accompanying lesson plans and ideas about engaging students in scientific inquiry. These are critical resources for schools that have limited funds available with which to purchase expensive equipment or to provide lab experiences for students.

TEACHING SOCIAL STUDIES

Social studies is the most challenging of the content areas for ELLs, both because of assumptions about the background knowledge students possess and because of the abstract nature of vocabulary and concepts used in the social studies classroom. It is easier to use visuals to demonstrate a mathematics operation or a scientific procedure than it is to visually depict concepts such as democracy, freedom of the press, or the causes of the Revolutionary War.

In addition, traditional social studies teaching is dependent upon the extensive reading of texts crammed with facts, names, places, and dates. When college students are surveyed about their school experiences in social studies and history classes, all too often they comment on all the boring information they were forced to memorize. On the other hand, social studies can be the most interesting and valuable subject to teach because of the possibility of engaging in culturally responsive pedagogy and promoting cross-cultural understanding. Social studies also has value in building on the funds of knowledge of families and communities, thereby affirming what children have learned from their experiences and enhancing self-concept.

Teaching social studies lessons in the L1 can have many benefits for the subsequent development of the L2. One example of this is the many cognates that can be found in both Spanish (and other romance languages) and English within the texts and materials used to teach social studies. For example, many of the words that end in *ión* in Spanish, such as *constitución, revolución, inmigración,* and *declaración,* have English counterparts. Other common cognates from social studies include words such as *conquistador, gobernador, presidente, parlamento, corte suprema, hemisferio, continente,* and *nativos.* Students who learn social studies lessons in Spanish and are taught to recognize the English equivalents of cognates will be better prepared to read English language texts when they make that transition.

Another critical value of social studies is the possibility it offers for integration with other content areas, such as language arts and fine arts, enabling a thematic approach to teaching. In the No Child Left Behind era, with its narrow focus on reading and mathematics, the social studies have received less prominence in the curriculum. Teachers often complain of too little time to teach social studies and too little support from administrators in doing so because of the pressure to raise standardized test scores in reading and math. However valid that critique, this argument ignores the wealth of literature for children and young adults that can be used to teach social studies concepts while literacy is being developed and while language arts are being taught. In addition, many themes that are part of the social studies curriculum are also found in child and adolescent literature.

TRY THIS!

Upper Elementary Level

Immigration is an important theme in social studies. How and why immigrants came to this country, how they adjusted, how their lives in their old homes differed from their lives in their new one, and how they contributed to the development of America are all a part of social studies. Identify a variety of children's literature that addresses this theme—including a selection of literature that has children from a background similar to those in your classes. Don't forget to include literature about African Americans who moved north from the South and were part of the Great Migration of African Americans. Such a theme can be enhanced by the use of oral history projects where children can interview an older member of a community, whether it is a grandparent or older relative, a storeowner, a local librarian, or a minister. They can find out things such as why the families of the interviewees came to this country (or, in the case of African Americans, why they migrated north), where they originated from, and how the schools and neighborhoods of origin were different from the new ones they encountered. Have children compare and contrast the stories they uncover from those that they read about in professionally published literature.

Social studies can also be a powerful content area in which to explore connections between people of differing backgrounds. The vignette below illustrates how connections can be forged between bilingual and mainstream classrooms through the theme of immigration:

Kathleen and Marlene had been teaching their African American fourth graders about the Great Migration of African Americans from the South to Chicago during the early 20th century. Both teachers were using children's books such as *The Great Migration*. Tina and Lisa had been teaching their Latino students about Mexican immigration. Both teachers were using children's books such as *Esperanza Rising*. To build upon their creative approaches, a project was developed to explore resources that teachers could use so that African American and Latino children could make connections between the experiences of migration and immigration of both groups. "Making Connections Between Black and Brown" demonstrated that there are many children's books that can help teachers address social studies while also teaching literacy and language arts. (Olmedo, 2006)

In addressing social studies concepts, teachers should also recognize the importance and value of using graphic organizers. Venn diagrams are especially valuable for helping ELLs compare and contrast historical events without needing to use too much written language. Anticipation guides can also have students make predictions about various events in history that they can later check for accuracy through evidence from various sources.

INTEGRATING THE CONTENT AREAS

Often, teachers will complain that, with pressures from standardized assessments and with teaching reading and mathematics skills, the areas that "count" most for accountability, there is not enough time to teach social studies and science, let alone music and art. For this reason, a thematic approach to instruction merits further discussion; it provides teachers with an opportunity to integrate knowledge and skills from language arts, mathematics, social studies, science, art, and even music into organized units. The unit on The Great Migration that Kathleen and Marlene were teaching (in the previous Try This! section) employed a thematic approach. The students were engaged in multiple learning activities. They were developing their literacy skills by reading a variety of fiction and nonfiction books and by interviewing parents and community members and then writing their stories. The students were also learning about the historical period and the geography of the migration route from the South to the North. The arts were incorporated as well. Kathleen and Marlene's students were engaged in critiquing the artwork of the era and in creating original artwork based upon the same style. They listened to musical styles of the era and participated in classroom skits in which they acted out characters from the literature they were reading or from the artworks they were viewing and creating. The teachers saw the connections between social studies and language arts and believed that it was possible to teach skills from both areas during the same time frame.

Learning through a thematic approach is especially valuable for emergent bilinguals because it not only facilitates vocabulary development, but also allows information to be repeated across subject areas with greater focus than might be the case if no effort was made to relate one subject to another. This can provide greater depth in what is taught since it is possible to devote more time to particular topics than to teaching some areas in isolation.

ADAPTING AVAILABLE MATERIALS

The availability of native language materials does not eliminate the need for teachers to use literacy skills similar to those used by teachers instructing English-proficient children. In those mainstream classes, teachers still need to explain new vocabulary words and help students use them, they need to help children read for comprehension and explain what they have read, and they need to help students infer the meaning of words from their context. Teachers also have to determine whether the readability level of the native language materials is appropriate for their students or if adaptations are in order due to material that is too advanced.

Whether in the native language or in English, teachers may need to make significant adjustments in the reading content and educational materials. It is critical that the reading that ELLs are asked to cover in order to learn math, science, and social studies be comprehensible. Students should not need to look up every other word in a glossary or a dictionary to figure out what the text says—this is a sure way to crush motivation. Anyone who has studied a foreign language recognizes the limitations of dictionaries when trying to understand a passage in that language. Not only is it a slow and laborious process; it also fails to promote learning new vocabulary in a realistic and communicative manner. Furthermore, since language is constantly evolving, students need to develop the skills needed to understand neologisms (new words) that they might not yet find in a dictionary.

Adaptations in textual materials may include those that pose cultural or experiential challenges and those that pose linguistic challenges. For example, native English-speaking children who have lived in the United States may have little difficulty in understanding a passage that speaks about the West Coast or the Midwest. Because of their cultural background or experiences, they may have a general idea of which states are being referred to or what areas of the country are involved. A child who does not speak English or who has not lived in the United States very long might not have any idea of where the Midwest or the West Coast are or what the terms even mean. These concepts would pose a cultural or experiential challenge for that child's understanding of the passage. Terms such as the *Fourth of July, Thanksgiving,* and other typical American holidays, may also have little meaning for such children and will need to be explained in a variety of ways. This is the case whether the children read these terms in their native language or in English.

Texts that pose linguistic challenges also need to be adapted. Most teachers are able to identify the specialized vocabulary that they need to teach in a passage, not only for ELLs but also for native English speakers. Occasionally, these terms are bolded in texts or found in a book's glossary. Linguistic challenges are also created, however, by idiomatic expressions that do not translate word for word across languages. Social studies texts in particular are filled with such expressions (e.g., *the king's subjects carried out the laws, the troops drove out the enemy, the head of government was forced out of office*). Other linguistic challenges include the passive versus the active voice, the presence of subordinate clauses, and complex verb structures. Teachers may find that reading aloud occasionally and paraphrasing some of these expressions can facilitate comprehension. They might also find it useful to teach *signal words* or *logical connectors*, which denote specific relationships such as *cause and effect, sequence, compare,* and *contrast*. Examples include *therefore, consequently, just as,* and *on the other hand* (which is also an idiomatic expression).

Some teachers may be fortunate enough to have access to content area materials in the students' native language. Several textbook companies publish social studies and language arts programs in Spanish, for example, and some districts provide these for classrooms. But even with access to materials in the L1, teachers need to make adaptations to take into account specialized vocabulary, students' L1 reading skills, and varieties of language used in the materials. Teachers cannot assume that just because the materials are written in the students' native language, the students will understand what is being written. This is especially the case if they have not been exposed to reading in their native language, as may have been true for many who received most or all of their instruction in U.S. schools. Even in cases where children were schooled in another country, the variety of language spoken in the home may deviate significantly from the standard variety of the language used in academic materials.

ADDITIONAL CONSIDERATIONS FOR TEACHING BILINGUALLY

In this chapter, we have discussed a variety of questions and approaches that bilingual teachers can use to teach mathematics, science, and social studies, whether in the L1 or the L2. These approaches include the following:

- Recognizing and teaching the specialized language of the content area
- Addressing the cultural or experiential and linguistic challenges of texts by reading aloud and paraphrasing passages

- Using a thematic approach to teaching content
- Providing hands-on materials for active learning
- Employing graphic organizers for teaching and assessment so as to limit the amount of written text that students have to process
- Using the native language where feasible and appropriate
- Maximizing the use of sheltered English when necessary to make the content comprehensible and insuring that content area teaching is not delayed until students have enough fluency in English

Teachers in a bilingual classroom who have the opportunity to teach content in the native language before students are transitioned into an English-only program may need to re-educate themselves in the academic language of their students' L1 for teaching purposes. Many bilingual teachers have not learned content through the minority language and may therefore be lacking that academic terminology themselves. If they do not know the appropriate vocabulary in the L1 of the students, how can they expect the students to use it in their explanations? Such teachers are challenged to be language models in both languages—the L1 of the student (the language spoken at home) and English, a theme to be taken up in the subsequent chapter.

Return to the Essential Question

What approaches should teachers consider for teaching content to English language learners in bilingual classrooms?

Monica reported that her eighth-grade Spanish/English bilingual students were engaged beyond her expectations when she taught a social studies unit on immigration from a critical pedagogical stance. She noted that even though it was the end of the academic year and her students were ready to graduate and move on to high school, they were not only attentive, but also sought to extend the learning beyond what was required. A powerful example of what can happen when teachers tap student background and engage their intellect in relevant ways was illustrated when one student traveled around school with a video recorder in order to document teacher, staff, and student feelings about the issues the class had been discussing.

It is not necessary for teachers to postpone the teaching of math, science, and social studies until that future time when their ELLs know enough English to access the curriculum through English-only approaches. Students must be taught these content areas and helped to tackle them through a variety of pedagogical approaches. Teaching the content in the students' home language is one approach facilitated by transitional and developmental bilingual education or dual language programs. Native-language teaching can help ELLs not only to access the concepts at an age-appropriate level, but also to develop literacy skills, such as the recognition and use of cognates, which will be essential when students are transitioned into the English classroom. Sheltered English instruction, in which English is modified to make concepts more comprehensible, can also be beneficial, but these approaches may not be productive before students reach an intermediate level of English language competency. Culturally relevant and critical pedagogy also can make a difference in student engagement with curriculum. An important concern is that teachers must recognize that children need to read to learn and not only learn to read. If they are going to be exposed to grade-level curricular content, teachers cannot wait until English language fluency has been achieved. Capitalizing on the skills that children bring with them from their home and community, especially their native language, maximizes the instructional time for the learning of academic concepts while the children are learning English. Such an approach can help facilitate a more productive transition to English when that becomes necessary. Another important transition in the content areas occurs for both students and teachers alike: the transition between vocabulary in the L1 and the L2. That is the subject of the next chapter.

REFERENCES

Cummins, J. (1991). Interdependence of first and second language proficiency in bilingual children. In E. Bialystok (Ed.), *Language processing in bilingual children* (pp. 70–89). Cambridge, MA: Cambridge University Press.

Freire, P., & Macedo, D. (1987). *Literacy: Reading the word and the world.* Hadley, MA: Bergin & Harvey.

Gutstein, E. (2003). Home buying while brown and black: Teaching mathematics for racial justice. *Rethinking Schools: An Urban Educational Journal, 18*(1), 35–37.

Gutstein, E., & Peterson, B. (2005). *Rethinking mathematics: Teaching social justice by the numbers.* Milwaukee, WI: Rethinking Schools.

Licon-Khisty, L., & Viego, G. (1999). Challenging conventional wisdom: A case study. In W. G. Secada (Ed.), *Changing the faces of mathematics: Pespectives on Latinos* (pp. 71–80). Reston, VA: National Council of Teachers of Mathematics.

Moll, L. (2005). *Funds of knowledge: Theorizing practices in households, communities, and classrooms.* Hillsdale, NJ: Erlbaum.

Olmedo, I. M. (2005). The bilingual echo: Bilingual children as language mediators in a dual language school. In M. Farr (Ed.), *Latino language and literacy in ethnolinguistic Chicago* (Vol. II). Hillsdale, NJ: Erlbaum.

Olmedo, I. M. (2006). Creating contexts for studying history with students learning English. In B. Lanman & L. Wendling (Eds.), *Preparing the next generation of oral historians: An anthology of oral history education.* Lanham, MD: Rowman & Littlefield.

5

Content and Professional Vocabulary Development

By contributing author
Jaime J. Gelabert-Desnoyer

Graphics by Cory Dewald

Essential Question

How can I effectively develop vocabulary in the bilingual classroom?

One Teacher's Dilemma

Although my students who are future Spanish-English bilingual teachers are quite pleased with the quality of our university's bilingual education program in terms of theory and practice, they often complain that they are not being adequately equipped with the Spanish vocabulary they will need in order to teach in the content areas. This includes pedagogical grammar—for example, the vocabulary they will need to teach mathematical operations, content vocabulary, and the technical scientific words they will need to teach about global warming in science class.

O ne of the most pressing issues bilingual teachers face in the United States is bridging the gap between their linguistic abilities in the native language of their students and the content knowledge of the subjects they teach. This is often most evident in the area of vocabulary, which often reveals inadequate preparation in both content and pedagogical vocabulary.

A considerable number of individuals who embark on the fascinating journey of becoming bilingual teachers have acquired their content knowledge and their linguistic skills in the L1 of their students separately. In other words, while these future educators show a high degree of linguistic competence in the L1 of their students, their vocabulary knowledge in specific areas (both content and pedagogical) may not be sufficient, in varying degrees and aspects, for the teaching skills they perform daily in the bilingual classroom. The purpose of this chapter is to provide support to bilingual educators in creating a learning environment in which content vocabulary is one of the main columns that supports instruction in the students' L1 and in which competence in their native language, including pedagogical vocabulary, is not only pragmatically relevant but also socially and culturally necessary. This chapter provides the bilingual teacher with clear, easy-to-follow guidelines to help integrate appropriate materials into the curriculum in order to improve vocabulary learning. The frequent use of semantic maps is a pedagogical tool that helps organize information visually and is ideal for working with vocabulary in the second language classroom, where visuals often shelter instruction. Examples of two semantic maps that highlight common topics in basic science and math at the elementary and middle school levels are included. A sample of vocabulary in English and Spanish is provided as a suggestion to help teachers create their own vocabulary lists.

It is important for the teacher to emphasize the notion that building vocabulary knowledge does not consist of merely adding single, discrete items to a list. When dealing with vocabulary, a large number of teachers now understand the importance of bringing to the classroom the five Cs (*Communication, Culture, Connections with other disciplines, Comparisons with students' native languages and cultures*, and *use of the foreign language in Communities outside the classroom*; see Haas, 2000). The application of these principles ideally results in an approach to understanding and building vocabulary knowledge that is a creative, open-ended process of constant evaluation. This has the added benefit of facilitating the assessment of the needs and peculiarities of the class at hand and is accomplished by considering the level of the course, the content (topic) at hand, and the desired depth (namely, the range of detail of the learned vocabulary).

SEMANTIC MAPS

Literature on the use of semantic maps as a pedagogical tool in education is robust (see Brown, 2002; Edens & Potter, 2003; Gómez, Moreno, Pazos, & Sierra-Alonso, 2000; Gordon, 2000; Novak, Gowin, & Johansen, 1983; Preece, 1999; Romance & Vitale, 1999). Semantic maps have also been used widely in other disciplines (for their application in psychology, see Goodyear, Tracey, Claiborn, Lichtenberg, & Wampold, 2005; for engineering, see Kramer, 1990; for science, see Robinson, 1999, and Slotte & Lonka, 1999; and for geology, see Verosub, 2000). Indeed, the diversity of fields that have used semantic maps and the interest concerning this technique have risen dramatically in the scientific community. This has resulted in many international conferences on the design and application of semantic mapping[1], where educators, businessmen, researchers in human and machine cognition, and scientists in general share their views on the issue.

A semantic map, as conceptualized by Novak in the 1970s (Novak, 1990), is essentially a pedagogical tool that organizes information visually and in a way that portrays at a glance the relationships between a central concept and other related secondary pieces of information. Because visuals can be an integral component of sheltered instruction, semantic maps have added significance for the second language learner. In this chapter, the general label *semantic maps* refers to both *mind maps* and *concept maps.* Although there is no general agreement on what constitutes each type of semantic map, it is generally assumed that a mind map differs in purpose from a concept map. The mind map displays a central concept from which secondary information branches off. This information may be of different kinds. It may refer to a class of objects (a general category, such as "means of motorized transportation" could generate *cars, speedboats,* and *planes*), properties (*rare, expensive,* and *hard* would stem from the term *diamond*) or examples (e.g., *Zimbabwe, Tanzania,* or *Algeria* could branch off from the category *African nations*). The second type of semantic map, the concept map, includes more than one concept, and its purpose is primarily to show the relationships between concepts or families of concepts and their similarities and disparities (e.g., systems of information processing, economic theories, political systems, and language acquisition hypotheses).

Both types of semantic maps share the characteristic of being pedagogical devices that are simple to create and use—a piece of paper and a pen is all that is needed—but that imply a great deal of planning and thinking. The process of deciding which are the primary, secondary, and subsequent pieces of information and what relationship they establish with the main concept demands a type of hierarchical thinking and

Elementary Level

Use the following maps with your students. The math map lays out the basic mathematical operations that students need to master. The map concerning the relationship between humans and the environment provides the student with a layout that is easy to follow and that can be used as a general template. These maps may be utilized in several ways. For teachers well in command of the students' native language, these semantic maps explain and aid in the retention of the materials to be taught. Students can check their knowledge of the topic by reproducing or simply keeping a copy of the whole map. Hulstijn (1997) and Novak (1990), among many other authors, note that this is one of the most powerful assets of the semantic map. For teachers who speak the students' native language but lack the lexical knowledge of the full extent of the lesson, the semantic map is used as a way to generate, in collaboration with students, the secondary vocabulary the class needs. Thus, while the teacher must know the basic concepts, other subsequent areas related to the core lesson are worked through as a joint effort with the students.

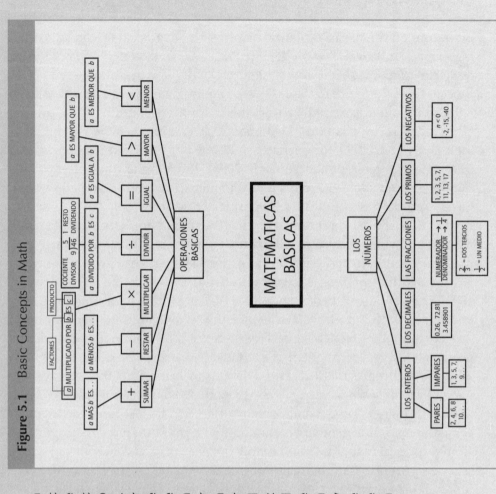

Figure 5.1 Basic Concepts in Math

Figure 5.2 How Humans Interact With Each Other and the Environment

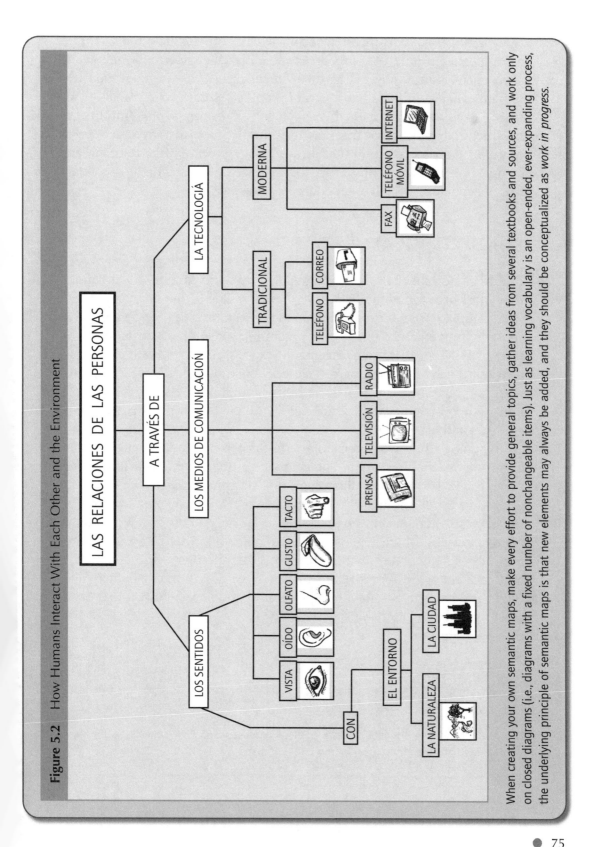

When creating your own semantic maps, make every effort to provide general topics, gather ideas from several textbooks and sources, and work only on closed diagrams (i.e., diagrams with a fixed number of nonchangeable items). Just as learning vocabulary is an open-ended, ever-expanding process, the underlying principle of semantic maps is that new elements may always be added, and they should be conceptualized as *work in progress*.

categorizing that is difficult to achieve with other study tools. This is accomplished through the process of the initial display of information and subsequent rearranging of the data. In this sense, it can be argued that semantic maps, unlike other forms of graphic displays of information, are truly sequential in their arrangement. By appearing initially as unstructured (in the sense that only the central topic is displayed at the very center of the page or computer screen[2]), they promote free thinking and compel the author of the map to organize and categorize secondary components from which other concepts will spring.

BUILDING VOCABULARY

Building vocabulary in the class must be, first and foremost, a collaborative effort between students and the teacher. One of the main benefits of decreasing the role of the teacher as the only source of knowledge is that students immediately feel a direct, genuine sense of accountability and responsibility for their own learning. In short, students cease to play a passive role in the class as mere recipients of knowledge. Using semantic maps as a pedagogical tool to identify, gather, and classify vocabulary items emphasizes creativity and collaboration between all participants, students and teacher alike.

When deciding what vocabulary best accommodates the needs of the classroom, every effort should be made to emphasize that learning vocabulary, unlike learning the phonological or morphological system of a language, is a never-ending process. This means that no one is an expert in all fields. A mathematician, for example, may only know a few words of astronomical vocabulary because the language of science is vast and ever expanding. Thus, more than focusing on discrete items, students in this approach are given appropriate tools that, ideally, will enable them to map out lexical items in any field of their interest and successfully understand, at a glance, the relationships between them.

TRY THIS!

Elementary Level

Use these basic-level vocabulary lists (in math, geometry, and measurement) with your students; have them turn the lists into semantic maps.

Basic math

Números	
Numbers	
Pares (dos, cuatro, seis)	
Even (two, four, six)	
Impares (uno, tres, cinco)	
Odd	
Enteros	
Whole numbers	
Ordinales (primero, segundo ...)	
Ordinal (first, second...)	
Negativos (menos uno: −1)	
Negative (minus one: −1)	
Operaciones	
Operations	
Adición	**Uno y tres son cuatro**
Addition	*One plus three equals four*
Sustracción	**Diez menos dos son ocho**
Subtraction	*Ten minus two equals eight*
Division	**Ocho dividido por cuatro es dos**
Division	*Eight divided by four equals two*
Multiplicación	**Seis por cinco son treinta**
Multiplication	*Six times five equals thirty*
Factores	
Factors	
Producto	
Product / result	
Tabla de multiplicación	
Multiplication chart	

(Continued)

(Continued)

Geometría *Geometry*	
Punto *Point*	
Línea *Line*	**Horizontal** *Horizontal*
	Vertical *Vertical*
	Diagonal *Diagonal*
	Paralelas *Parallel*
	Cruzadas *Intersecting*
Ángulo *Angle*	**Recto** *Right*
	Agudo *Acute*
	Obtuso *Obtuse*
	Llano *Straight*
Polígonos *Polygons*	**Triángulo** *Triangle*
	Cuadrilátero *Quadrilateral*
	Pentágono *Pentagon*
	Hexágono *Hexagon*
	Heptágono *Heptagon*
	Octágono *Octagon*
	Decágono *Decagon*
	Dodecágono *Dodecagon*

Measurements

Tiempo *Time*	Segundos *Seconds*
	Minutos *Minutes*
	Horas *Hours*
	Días *Days*
	Semanas *Weeks*
	Meses *Months*
	Años *Years*
	Décadas *Decades*
	Siglos *Centuries*
	Millenio (milenios) *Millennium (millenia)*
Temperatura *Temperature*	Grados *Degrees*
	Fahrenheit Celsius
	Náutica *Nautic*
	Terrestre *Land*
Longitud *Length*	
Inglesas (English)	Pulgada *Inch*
	Pie *Foot*
	Yarda *Yard*
	Milla *Mile*

(Continued)

(Continued)

Métrica (metric)	Milímetro *Millimeter*
	Centímetro *Centimeter*
	Metro *Meter*
	Decámetro *Decameter*
	Hectómetro *Hectometer*
	Kilómetro *Kilometer*

TRY THIS!

Secondary Level

Use the vertebrate animals (zoology) vocabulary list with your students; have them turn the list into a semantic map.

ANIMALES VERTEBRADOS *Vertebrate Animals*	
Rasgos generales *General traits*	Tienen They have
	Cabeza *Head*
	Tronco *Torso*
	Extremidades *Limbs*

Tipos _Types_	
Peces _Fish_	**Branquias** _Gills_
	Escamas _Scales_
Anfibios _Amphibians_	**Pulmones** _Lungs_
	Piel _Skin_
Reptiles _Reptiles_	**Pulmones** _Lungs_
	Escamas _Scales_
Aves _Birds_	**Pulmones** _Lungs_
	Plumas _Feathers_
Mamíferos _Mammals_	**Pulmones** _Lungs_
	Pelo Fur

INTEGRATING SEMANTIC MAPS IN THE CLASSROOM

The following suggestions, inspired by Zaid (1995), are intended to provide a blueprint of how semantic maps may be integrated in the classroom.

1. Identify the topic
    Begin by identifying the general topic that will be discussed. Remember, semantic maps are generally divided into mind maps (one single topic) and concept maps (several interrelated topics). Depending on

the topic to be discussed, identify which type of map is more suitable for the vocabulary to be studied.

2. Brainstorm basic semantic relations

After the general topic has been decided, every semantic map should start with a brainstorming session. The students and teacher decide during class which items will be needed in the particular lesson for the instructional topic (e.g., kinship relations, the animal kingdom and its subspecies, basic concepts in mathematics, ethnic groups around the world). Perhaps one of the most valuable ingredients in working with semantic maps is the playful, low-stress environment created (also known as a "low affective filter"; see Krashen & Terrell, 1983). The teacher (or a volunteer) draws on the board and has the students suggest (by way of free association) the pertinent secondary concepts. Once the central topic and the main secondary branches have been laid out, the teacher breaks the class up into groups of students (two to four would be ideal) who have to hunt for the lexical items pertinent to the branch they have been assigned by using primary and secondary sources, dictionaries, and other appropriate materials to fill in their part of the map. This can be done in class or as homework. This stage of the elaboration of a semantic map may be accomplished in a computer lab where students have quick, easy access to online dictionaries and pictures of the items.

3. Understand the significance of regionalisms/synonyms

In specialized or general scientific language, some synonyms may have virtually the same meaning, even though their use may differ contextually. For example, *cold* and *frigid* may have virtually the same meaning, but the two terms are not interchangeable in all contexts. These differences are often language specific. Spanish, unlike English, differentiates between live fish (*pez:* singular, *peces:* plural) and caught fish, which are categorized as food (*pescado*). English distinguishes between *pig* and *pork,* the latter referencing its status as a type of meat. Spanish does not differentiate between the two; indeed, there are many other names in Spain and Latin America that may be used interchangeably to refer to the animal as well as the meat: *cerdo, puerco, gorrino, marrano, cuino, chancho, guarro,* and so on.

A comprehensive semantic map, consequently, should not only map the literal meaning of a word, but should also reflect—to the extent appropriate for the level and purpose of the class—this lexical and cultural diversity. In this sense, semantic maps are an excellent tool for incorporating the many different layers of meaning and possible usages for words.

This ability is further emphasized by using pictures and different font sizes and colors to link the different branches. Once again, this is a highly individual process in which students are free to work on the semantic maps in whatever way feels natural to them.

INCORPORATING THE FIVE Cs AND OTHER LINGUISTIC VARIETIES IN SEMANTIC MAPS

When students work directly with semantic maps, it is important to incorporate as many of the Five Cs as possible. This may be easily accomplished by extending the connections that are already present in the semantic maps that students are creating. For example, if the class is working with vocabulary about farm animals, the teacher can have students research the literary forms (e.g., stories, plays, tales, songs, and fables such as *The Three Pigs*) where this vocabulary appears. It might be even more informative to have students ask members of their families about the structure or narrative of the tale, story, or song. Do all of their families know the tale in the same way? Are there stories, superstitions, or folk tales that are unique to any culture or background present in the classroom?

After mapping the lexical items studied in the class, further connections may be investigated. In what other fields of knowledge, such as science or industry, are those words used? Establishing links between lexical items and other fields where the words are present emphasizes an understanding of interconnectedness.

ASSESSMENT USING CONCEPT MAPS

A great advantage of concept maps is that they simplify (in terms of both time and effort) the task of assessing what the student understands and is capable of recalling. In fact, semantic maps were initially devised by Novak as a way of assessing students' compositions (in Clariana, Koul, & Salehi, 2006). When a teacher needs to check comprehension as well as retention, concept maps provide an effective, economical, and simple tool for evaluating the level of the class. (See McLure et al., 1999, or Ruíz-Primo & Shavelson, 1996, for a discussion of assessment of science education through concept maps.) Because of their schematic nature (i.e., concepts are printed in the form of keywords rather than in full, written sentences), they are easy to reproduce in the class, and retention is improved if the first step in creating the semantic maps—brainstorming—is repeated. As

Webb (2007) has pointed out, repetition is an essential aspect in vocabulary learning, both in the L1 and the L2.

DEVELOPMENT OF PEDAGOGICAL GRAMMAR IN THE EDUCATOR'S L2

When the bilingual teacher lacks elementary content knowledge in the students' L1, he or she must make every effort to become familiar with the ways in which content knowledge is introduced in pedagogical materials designed with the native speaker in mind. Thus, it is an essential task to analyze how concepts (in math, science, geography, and other content areas) are presented in textbooks in the students' native language, even in elementary picture books, educational videos, and Web sites. At the crux of the problem are the numerous expressions that are either unknown by the teacher or use cognates that are misleading in their meaning. For example, many mathematical and scientific terms are identical (division = *división*, multiplication = *multiplicación*, alliteration = *aliteración*, plantigrade = *plantígrado*), while others are completely different (billion = *mil millones* [or *millardo*], billion = *trillón*, walrus = *morsa*, etc). It is vital, then, that the teacher checks thoroughly the possible mismatches of the vocabulary that she or he plans to use in the classroom, always taking into account the level and background knowledge of the students.

Concept mapping is, again, a great tool for educators to use in organizing information for themselves. Teachers are encouraged to create and review their own maps often in internalizing concepts and relationships between concepts.

Return to the Essential Question

How can I effectively develop vocabulary in the bilingual classroom?

One Teacher's Response

If you're teaching new vocabulary in a dual language setting, it shouldn't be a two-day lesson thing. It should be more extended. It should go more into the concepts.

César, a Spanish bilingual teacher, validates the teaching of vocabulary as extended and conceptual. Teaching content vocabulary in the native language of bilingual students can be somewhat problematic. Yet the very need to bridge the gap between what teachers know and what they need to know may bring students and teachers together in the use of a pedagogical tool that is highly appropriate when teaching and learning vocabulary. Semantic maps are efficient because they are based on associating principles and concepts. Thus they become an ideal instrument for connecting the literary (descriptive) meaning of discrete lexical items with other relevant information.

Semantic maps have proven their efficacy in both teaching and learning. Even the most useful tool, however, can fail to promote learning if the classroom environment is not one of respect and collaboration. In this sense, the lack of lexical preparation that many bilingual education teachers perceive within themselves should be regarded as a valuable opportunity for growth. Understanding that lexical knowledge is an open-ended process of continuous learning, the teacher may use the techniques mentioned in this chapter to construct a classroom where learning is a dynamic, collaborative, and engaging process. Just as semantic maps have proven their efficacy in building vocabulary, there are proven techniques for integrating second language instruction with other aspects of learning. This is the subject of Chapter 6.

NOTES

1. These conferences started in 2004 at the Universidad Pública de Navarra (Spain) and the 2008 meeting was in Helsinki (Finland) and Tallinn (Estonia), September 22–25.

2. There are currently numerous software programs designed for concept mapping: e.g., MindTools, iMindMap, Visual Mind.

REFERENCES

Brown, D. A. (2002). Creative concept mapping. *The Science Teacher, 69*(3), 58–61.

Clariana, R., Koul, R., & Salehi, R. (2006). The criterion-related validity of a computer-based approach for scoring concept maps. *The International Journal of Instructional Media, 33*(3), 317–325.

Edens, K. M., & Potter, E. (2003, March). Using descriptive drawings as a conceptual change strategy in elementary science. *School Science and Mathematics, 103*(3), 135–144.

Gómez, A., Moreno, A., Pazos, J., & Sierra-Alonso, A. (2000). Knowledge maps: An essential technique for conceptualization. *Data and Knowledge Engineering, 33*(2), 169–190.

Goodyear, R. K., Tracey, T. J. G., Claiborn, C. D., Lichtenberg, J. W., & Wampold, B. E. (2005). Ideographic concept mapping in counseling psychology research: Conceptual overview, methodology, and an illustration. *Journal of Counseling Psychology, 52*(2), 236–242.

Gordon, J. L. (2000). Creating knowledge maps by exploiting dependent relationships. *Knowledge-Based Systems, 13*(2–3), 71–79.

Haas, M. (2000, September). Thematic, communicative language teaching in the K–8 classroom. *Center for Applied Linguistics.* Retrieved June 10, 2008, from http://www.cal.org/resources/Digest/0004thenatic.html

Hulstjin, J. (1997). Mnemonic methods in foreign language vocabulary learning: Theoretical considerations and pedagogical implications. In J. Coady & T. Huckin (Eds.), *Second language vocabulary acquisition.* (pp. 203–224). Cambridge, MA: Cambridge University Press.

Kramer, S. (1990). Application of concept mapping to systems engineering. Proceedings of the IEEE International Conference on Systems, Man and Cybernetics, 652–654.

Krashen, S. D., & Terrell, T. D. (1983). *The natural approach: Language acquisition in the classroom.* London: Prentice Hall Europe.

McClure, J. R., Sonak, B., Suen, H. K. (1999). Concept map assessment of classroom learning: Reliability, validity, and logistical practicality. *Journal of Research in Science Teaching, 36*(4), 475–492.

Novak, J. D. (1990). Concept mapping: A useful tool for science education. *Journal of Research in Science Teaching, 27*(10), 937–949.

Novak, J. D., Gowin, D. B., & Johansen, G. T. (1983). The use of concept mapping and knowledge: Vee mapping with junior high school science students. *Science Education, 67*(5), 625–645.

Preece, P. F. W. (1999). Review of learning, creating, and using knowledge: Concept maps as facilitative tools in schools and corporations. *British Journal of Educational Psychology, 69*(1), 128–129.

Robinson, W. R. (1999). A view from the science education research literature: Concept map assessment of classroom learning, *Journal of Chemical Education, 76*(9), 1179–1180.

Romance, N. R., & Vitale, M. R. (1999, Spring). Concept mapping as a tool for learning. *College Teaching, 47*(2), 74–79.

Ruíz-Primo, M. A., & Shavelson, R. J. (1996). Problems and issues in the use of concept maps in science assessment. *Journal of Research in Science Teaching, 33*(6), 569–600.

Slotte, W., & Lonka, K. (1999). Spontaneous concept maps aiding the understanding of scientific concepts. *International Journal of Science Education, 21*(5), 515–531.

Verosub, K. L. (2000, November). A mind-map of geology. *Journal of Geoscience Education, 48*(5), 599.

Webb, S. (2007). The effects of repetition on vocabulary knowledge. *Applied Linguistics 28*(1), 46–65.

Zaid, M. A. (1995, July–September). Semantic mapping in communicative language teaching. *English Teaching Forum, 33*(3), Retrieved June 2, 2008, from http://forum.state.gov/vols/vol33/no3/p6.htm

6 Second Language Instruction

Essential Question

Do I need to have a separate time slot for teaching English as a second language?

One Teacher's Dilemma

We want them to be successful in both languages, so you have to give them the time to do it, and they're capable of doing it. And I think that the end result is a tremendous effort for them. A lot of times I feel bad because they're not getting credit for that. I have kids who are publishing in both English and Spanish, and I feel so proud of them.

Araceli feels the press of time in her Spanish bilingual classroom. Her dilemma is not unusual. Bilingual teachers are responsible for the same curriculum as mainstream teachers, yet they have the additional responsibility of facilitating second language development in their students. How is it possible to accomplish all of this in the same classroom hours that other teachers have for a more limited curriculum? Increasingly, educators are looking to the integration of language and content as a way to more effectively teach language while reducing the need to devote as much time to language as a separate subject. The teaching of English as only a separate subject taught by an ESL specialist in a pull-out program model is increasingly being called into question as more emphasis is placed on the integration of language and content learning. This chapter addresses contemporary methods and strategies for teaching English. While the focus is on teaching English as a second or other language, most of the information in this chapter can be applied to the learning of languages other than English.

SHELTERING AND SCAFFOLDING INSTRUCTION FOR EMERGENT BILINGUAL STUDENTS

> I want the kids to understand that we are serious about language policy in our school. They need to use what they learn; if they don't use it, then what's the point of being in a bilingual program?

Spanish bilingual teacher Dolores realizes that language and education policy need to be reflected at the local school level. In order to bridge policy to practice, bilingual teachers have some specific strategies available to them. Sheltering and scaffolding are two modifications to instructional practice that are essential to assisting students' L2 development and making the curriculum accessible. Sheltered instruction accomplishes this by focusing on the use of the following:

- *Comprehensible input,* or the continuous modification of teacher speech to facilitate the development of the students' L2
- Visuals, including pictures, graphs, and charts, to assist in explaining concepts
- Context-embedded instruction (instruction based in authentic experiences)
- Communicative opportunities in the social environment

Comprehensible input is the receptive form of language. Since the primary source of comprehensible input to ELLs (while in the classroom) is the teacher, teachers must take special care to ensure that their use of English is understood by the students. The primary means of doing so is through the modification of teacher talk, using techniques such as gesture, facial expression, rate of speech (but not volume), sentence expansion, repetition, and thoughtfully placed pauses. However, the idea behind comprehensible input is not to over-simplify, but rather to amplify: to say the same thing in different ways to provide multiple points of entry (Walqui & van Lier, 2009).

Comprehensible output is expressive. It is not just student talk in the L2 (English); it is also the ability to communicate in English with native English speakers. Comprehensible input is a prerequisite for comprehensible output. It is important not to expect comprehensible output from students until they have received enough comprehensible input. Furthermore, it is important to recognize that a silent period normally precedes comprehensible output. Do not assume that ELLs are not actively engaged in learning if they are initially silent in the L2. If comprehensible input is being provided, they are more than likely developing their L2 skills as they listen. However, while students may be learning when they are listening, it is also important to scaffold instruction so that even beginners can participate and speak during class. In other words, student learning during the silent period cannot be taken for granted, but should be fostered through thoughtful planning and strategizing.

To clarify appropriate second language levels (whether in English for ELLs or another language for native speakers of English), in this chapter we use the label *L2 Level* and specify whether activities are best used at the beginner, intermediate, or advanced level, or at multiple levels. We use *beginner* to refer to students who have little to no background in the language and can only use it for the most basic social purposes. *Intermediate* refers to students who are comfortable using the L2 for social purposes and have basic vocabulary development. *Advanced* refers to students who are more comfortable with the L2 not only for social purposes, but to a large extent for academic purposes as well. Yet advanced-level second language students still require academic language and literacy support. Beginners cannot yet maximize the benefits of sheltered instruction. Intermediates have reached the stage where sheltered instruction becomes useful. Advanced students are transitioning to the point where they can benefit from mainstream instruction. Ideally, however, they should continue to develop their L1 language and literacy.

In the example that follows, you can see how the use of a wordless book with vibrant, imaginative, engaging illustrations shelters L2 comprehension and encourages comprehensible output, first orally and then in written form, with students who have received sufficient comprehensible input. Notice how the social nature of the activity enhances student engagement. This activity is geared toward creating opportunities for comprehensible output and writing in the L2; thus it is appropriate for intermediate and advanced levels of second language learning.

> **TRY THIS!**
>
> **Lower Elementary Level**
>
> **Intermediate and Advanced L2 Level**
>
> Present the wordless book *Tuesday*, by David Wiesner (1991), to the class. In this lovely and inviting book, frogs on lily pads fly above a town each night, leaving behind mysterious clues that the townsfolk try to understand. The final picture in the book shows pigs flying in the night sky, but leaves the reader guessing as to what will happen next. As you display each picture, facilitate a class discussion in the L2 on what is happening in each illustration. Accept all reasonable responses, encourage multiple interpretations, and let the students know that they will soon have to decide within a group what is happening on each page. Divide the class into subgroups of approximately four students. Distribute post-its and pens or pencils, and ask each group to create simple text for each page using one post-it per page. Post the newly created text on each page. When all the groups have finished, have each group read the story (while displaying the illustrations) to the other groups. If student interest warrants it, lead the class in a discussion that compares and contrasts the various versions of the story.
>
> Imagining what happens when the story ends could extend this activity. (One logical extension could involve flying pigs taking over the town after the previous plague of frogs on flying lily pads.) Students could create the next book in the series, but this time they would have to create both the illustrations and the texts. If students are enthusiastic, this activity could extend into a whole series of books that could be published and displayed in the classroom library.

Other strategies for sheltering instruction include, but are not limited to, the following:

- Using concrete objects such as manipulatives (items that support hands-on learning), artifacts (something created by a student for a specific purpose), and realia (real objects used to convey meaning and add interest)
- Using pictures, graphs, charts, diagrams, photographs, and drawings
- Embedding instruction in real life activities, where the teacher can model what the students will be required to do

Another potent tool for making the L2 curriculum accessible to bilingual students is *scaffolding*. This is a way of providing support to students through modeling, feedback, instruction, and questioning. It is based on the premise that what the learner is able to do with assistance from the teacher and peers today, the learner can do alone tomorrow. Thus, the temporary supports that are provided by scaffolding are removed once they are no longer needed. For example, if primary-level students are using manipulatives to learn how to do mathematical equations in addition, once they have internalized the concept and can successfully write and complete addition equations on their own, the manipulatives are no longer required and, hence, no longer used.

Many of the activities in which you may already be engaging your bilingual students are based upon scaffolding techniques—even if you have not named them as such. For example, the writing process may begin with brainstorming rather than a "cold write." In this way, students think about writing in many ways, such as tapping prior knowledge or vivid imagining, before they put pen to paper. Initial drafts are shared and discussed in a social context before editing even begins. Breaking down writing into steps that build on one another is a natural and motivating way to scaffold writing. The steps that are taken in scientific inquiry work in much the same way. It is important to keep in mind that while some scaffolds are temporary, others are permanent. For example, math manipulatives should be removed when students internalize math concepts. In the writing process, on the other hand, steps such as brainstorming and drafting should remain as permanent features. In the example that follows, you can see one way scaffolding can work in math as students start with manipulatives and move toward writing an equation on paper.

TRY THIS!

Lower Elementary Level

Beginning and Intermediate L2 Level

Distribute dried beans or other manipulatives to the students. Begin by having the students count out the amount of beans called for by the teacher. After you (the teacher) have had each student count out six beans, ask how many groups of three can be made out of the six beans. Lead the class through multiple questions that are similar in nature. (For example, "Count 12 beans. How many groups of three can you make out of 12?") Introduce the symbol and the word for divide. The students should already be familiar with the sign for equal. Have them create *division pictures* by pasting beans on paper and writing the equation underneath. For example, in the equation $12 \div 3 = 4$, twelve beans would be pasted above the 12, three beans would be pasted above the 3, and four groups of three beans each would be pasted above the 4. Students could initially do this activity in groups, later in pairs, and finally individually. Each time the activity is done, the numbers could be changed. For example, students could group twenty beans into groups of five or sixteen beans into groups of four. At the completion of the activity, a variety of equations could be posted throughout the room.

In addition to using the writing process, scientific inquiry, and manipulatives, other activities that are easily scaffolded include the following:

Project-Based Learning

Elementary Through Secondary Level
Intermediate and Advanced L2 Level

According to Michael Simkins of the Multimedia Project (2000), project-based learning (PBL) "is a model for classroom activity that shifts away from the classroom practices of short, isolated, teacher-centered lessons and instead emphasizes learning activities that are long-term, interdisciplinary, student-centered, and integrated with real-world issues and practices." This type of learning allows students to follow their own interests, ask their own questions, and find their own answers while building positive relationships with their teachers, peers, and even the larger community.

Literature Circles

Upper Elementary and Secondary Level
Advanced L2 Level

Literature circles work much like book clubs do for adults. Students are allowed to pick the chapter book they would like to read as a small group—usually consisting of four to six students. Some educators suggest assigning specific roles to each member of the group to ensure that all students are focused and participating in the reading and conversation. The teacher is responsible for providing guidance and protocols for group discussions. When all of the literature circles in a classroom revolve around a common theme, it is possible to follow up with full group discussions in which the students compare and contrast the chapter books they have chosen to read and discuss with their respective groups.

Cooperative Learning

Elementary Through Secondary Level
Beginner, Intermediate, and Advanced L2 Level

In cooperative learning, groups of students work together to accomplish a common task. This can be accomplished through a variety of strategies, descriptions of which are readily available in many teacher texts and trade books. Because of the rich opportunities provided for small group verbal interactions, cooperative learning is especially helpful for ELLs when they are integrated in groups with native speakers of English. They are encouraged by the members of the group and can participate at their ability level. English language learners working in cooperative groups must be given assignments according to their levels of English proficiency, which requires that the teacher be aware of their stages of language acquisition.

The Language Experience Approach (LEA) as Modified for Use With ELLs

Lower Elementary Level
Beginner and Intermediate L2 Level

Reyes and Vallone (2008) describe the Language Experience Approach for ELLs as one in which "the class discusses a common experience they have shared as the teacher writes what the students dictate. For instance, in the younger grades, the teacher might schedule a class field trip that reinforces content, and then ask the children to write a story with him after returning to class. . . . [T]he teacher writes exactly what they say on a chart or on the board. Composing together, the teacher takes the opportunity to think out loud about their writing. For example, he might say, 'We want this sentence to show that we are excited. How do we accomplish this?' . . . If the students offer a grammatically incorrect response, the teacher may want to model his thinking in making the written correction" (p. 41). Be careful not to overcorrect, however. The type of developmental errors that a native English speaker might make will more than likely be naturally overcome in time. (For a discussion of extension activities for using the LEA with ELLs, see Reyes & Vallone, 2008, p. 41.)

INTEGRATING LANGUAGE, CONTENT, AND PROCESS

I try to connect English, I try to integrate English with whatever we are doing, either science or social studies. So, I guess, I started out doing a unit on feelings, and we basically did an alphabet book of feelings and we brainstormed. . . . So we did that unit, and we made an alphabet book and stuff like that, and I tried to bring in poetry and we talked about our feelings and also doing nice things for others and making them feel good . . . and they read the poems, they made up their own poems.

Jill, a bilingual teacher in a Spanish two-way immersion school, discusses how she integrates language and content for her Spanish-dominant students. Because she engages in constructivist practice, she integrates a process-oriented approach, in which emphasis is placed on the learning that occurs during the activity, rather than focusing solely on the final product. Scientific inquiry is an integral part of her science curriculum. Instead of reading about insects from a text, Jill brings captive bugs into her classroom and has the students chart their life cycles. She naturally integrates language, content, and process within her classroom. Just as language teachers integrate language and content, constructivist teachers integrate content and process. It is a natural extension for bilingual teachers with a constructivist perspective to integrate all three important elements. In the activity below, the integration of language, content, and process is highlighted within a science unit on plants. Rather than relying on a textbook with workbooks to teach English or science to ELLs, in this activity real plants are incorporated into the lesson. This technique, referred to as *context-embedded instruction,* aids student comprehension of both science vocabulary and grammatical structures in the L2, and the social nature of the activity lends itself to both comprehensible input and comprehensible output in the L2.

TRY THIS!

Upper Elementary Level

Beginning, Intermediate, and Advanced L2 Level

Bring a fully bloomed and easily seeded flowering annual from your geographic region into the classroom. Converse with the class about the stem, petals, leaves, pistil, and other parts of the plant, touching each named part. Let the students know that each of them will grow their own plant. Present and name the needed materials; soil, seeds, and paper cups. Discuss the elements needed for the plant to grow, such as sun and water. Provide pictures of these elements as visual aids. Guide students through the preparation and seeding of the soil and the placement of individually labeled paper cup pots in an appropriate area of the classroom (such as the windowsill). Display and discuss pictures of what can happen to seedlings and mature plants if they receive insufficient or excessive sun or water. Guide the students in beginning a plant journal in which they will describe the weekly progress of the plant as they care for it based upon directions on the seed packet. After the plant has bloomed, guide the students in creating charts that show the growth of the plant over time, based upon what they have noted in their plant journal. Discuss the findings with the entire group.

APPROPRIATE TIME FOR SECOND LANGUAGE INSTRUCTION IN A BILINGUAL CLASSROOM

> I just see my role as teaching them English as major, major. . . . I see that as the most important thing I have to do, to help them acquire the language. It's also what their parents want, and it's also what I want. So a major part of my teaching is on [English] language acquisition.

The role of the bilingual teacher in facilitating second language development is indeed crucial to the educational success of students and the viability of bilingual program models. Tung, a Chinese bilingual teacher, is keenly aware that the desire to assist students in reaching high levels of English proficiency is shared by parents and educators. Deciding exactly how to teach English, however, may be more complex than it sounds.

One of the first considerations should be whether ESL,[1] content-based English, or both, will be offered. The difference between ESL and content-based English (sheltered English) is the difference between teaching a second language and teaching content through a second language. In ESL, the primary goal is second language development. This may be done through a variety of approaches, some traditional (such as the audio-lingual approach) and some more natural (such as the communicative approach). In content-based English, teaching content through a second language is done through the use of sheltered techniques in the integration of the L2 and one of the content areas (or more if a thematic unit is used).

Sheltered English instruction is not very effective until the learner reaches an intermediate level of English language proficiency, when conversational English proficiency is achieved. At that point, sheltered instruction usually begins in math and science because these content areas are more easily contextualized (Crawford & Krashen, 2007).

Beginners—and especially newcomers—have much to gain from time that is focused on learning English. While time needs to be provided for both ESL and sheltered English content instruction at all levels, the lower the level of English proficiency, the more time should be devoted to ESL. Conversely, the higher the level of English proficiency, the more time should be devoted to sheltered content instruction. With more advanced students, sheltered English combined with mini-lessons on explicit language learning in accordance with student need might be sufficient. However, the type of L2 development needed by a given student is mediated by other variables, such as age, motivation, and the level of native language literacy of the learner.

The age of the learner is a crucial factor when deciding on how to approach second language development. With younger children, cognitive demands are lower. A five-year-old's English is far less complex than the English of a twelve-year-old. In addition, language learning easily lends itself to childhood songs, games, and the creative arts. The attention spans of younger children are shorter, which is another crucial factor in educational planning.

Older ELLs who enter the educational system with low levels of L2 proficiency will have more to learn and less time in which to learn it. This is compounded by the myriad amount of testing that is required of all students in public education, which takes away instructional time that could be used for both language and content learning. Students with limited English proficiency who enter the system at an older age need more time focused on explicit L2 instruction. They have less time in the school system in which to become proficient. The development of native language literacy should not be overlooked, however, because it can be a significant stepping-stone to English acquisition, contributing to the students' bilingualism and biliteracy. Some students may come from countries where they have little formal literacy education in their native language—hence, there will be less language transfer, and learning English will be more challenging. Others will arrive with high levels of literacy and academic achievement in their native language, facilitating language transfer. Students who have taken English as a foreign language (EFL) in high school may be eager language learners, motivated to partake in both natural and structured methods of developing their L2.

How much time should be given to second language instruction in a bilingual classroom? The answer to this question is complex. Generally, the way English is taught and the amount of time allocated to teaching it is mandated by state, district, or school policy. In the real world, more often it is left to chance rather than tailored to the needs of the students. Keep in mind that all ELLs need access to both L2 instruction (teaching language) and sheltered English instruction (teaching language through content). The more sheltered instruction offered during the instructional day, the more that English learning is maximized efficiently and effectively. However, this should not be done at the expense of native language literacy or cognitive and academic development. A healthy balance of L1 and L2 instruction must also be considered. Educational policies that mandate specific amounts of instructional time in each language should consider all of these important variables.

THE ROLE OF EXPLICIT LANGUAGE INSTRUCTION

All students come to the classroom with a great resource—language. Regardless of the variety they speak or whether they can read or write it, the language they bring is systematic and useful for communication. In a bilingual classroom, students are constantly acquiring language when it is used as the medium of instruction, but there are times when relying on implicit language learning is insufficient. Therefore, direct or explicit instruction must be an essential part of any bilingual education program. It offers students opportunities to understand the way language works as it highlights particularly challenging aspects of both oral and written language.

Over time, the approaches to language instruction have swung back and forth like a pendulum. At one end, the *direct grammar method* teaches language structures explicitly in isolation—a "drill-and-kill" approach. Students practice the same skill over and over without the need to understand or apply it to authentic situations. Many of us experienced this type of instruction in high school foreign language classes. By contrast, *communicative language learning* relies on natural and comprehensible input to implicitly transmit language structures (Krashen, 1985). There are also a variety of approaches, such as *focus on form*, that take more of a middle-ground approach. As bilingual educators, we need to take a both-and (rather than an either-or) approach to language instruction. Space should be created, where student need dictates, for explicit language instruction to support the understanding of language, and eventually content, as we continue to use and scaffold languages in our day-to-day content instruction.

A study on secondary long-term English learners, students who had been identified as ELLs for seven or more years in the United States, revealed a strong need for explicit literacy instruction (Menken, Kleyn, & Chae, 2007). This was found to be the case in both English and their native language.

While teachers at the secondary level often assume literacy skills, there is a need for explicit literacy instruction in the language arts and across the content areas. Since every subject has its own approach to reading and writing, there is a need to scaffold how to read and write in each area (Calderón, 2007). Think about the way you read in social studies versus the way you read a word problem in math; the focus and goal of each is quite different. In social studies, students generally need to read for larger concepts and ideas, whereas, for word problems in math, attention to detail is key, as is differentiating between salient and extraneous information. As a result, rather than just telling students to complete a given task, we need to make the process more explicit. Thus, all teachers must simultaneously become content and language teachers.

PROVIDING EXPLICIT LANGUAGE INSTRUCTION (INCLUDING GRAMMAR INSTRUCTION)

When it comes to teaching students a second language, the commonalities across oral and written aspects of languages can help us determine which linguistic features transfer from one language to the next. This means that students do not need to relearn a given concept because their understanding stays consistent from one language to the next. For example, between Spanish and English, students can transfer general sentence structure, many cognates, and most of the alphabet and its corresponding letter sounds. However, when there are aspects that differ from one language to the next, explicit instruction becomes necessary. For native Spanish speakers, teachers may need to discuss differences in punctuation, noun-adjective order, and the function of contractions in English. Korean speakers will need to learn that registers to indicate formality are expressed differently in English, and they will require an introduction to apostrophes and to the articles *the* and *a*, which are not part of the Korean language.

The goal of explicit instruction is to increase students' *metalinguistic awareness,* or the way they think about language. Since bilingual students are developing both languages, they have the benefit of using their entire linguistic repertoire for a basis of comparing and understanding the ways languages work. Similarly, as bilingual educators, your proficiency in the two languages is a considerable advantage in the determination of when explicit language instruction in English and the LOTE would benefit your students. Students' inherent awareness of two languages is made explicit as cognates are explored in the activity that follows. This activity does not involve teaching cognates; it merely enhances students' awareness of this natural linguistic scaffold.

TRY THIS!

Elementary and Secondary Level

Beginning, Intermediate, and Advanced L2 Level

Cognates are words with a common pronunciation or spelling and meaning between two languages. For example, *clima* (Spanish) and *climate,* or *utilize* (French) and *use* are cognates, whereas *carpeta* (Spanish for *folder*) and *carpet* are false cognates. If you teach in a language that shares many cognates with English, create a "Cognate Word Wall" in your classroom. Design two columns, one for cognates and another for false cognates. (These can also be referred to as friends and false friends for the lower grades.) Ask students to be on the lookout for (1) words that sound alike and have similar meanings across languages and (2) words that sound the same and have different meanings. Since many cognates are in the areas of content or technical vocabulary, making these connections is especially important in the upper grades, where students are exposed to more sophisticated concepts and language. In addition, all students will be able to see how knowing one language serves as an advantage as they learn another language.

Various perspectives exist on whether and how grammar should be taught. For example, a beginning language learner needs to spend more time on vocabulary development than grammar since it's very difficult to apply language functions and structures without a basic lexicon or word bank (Lewis, 1993). Simply relying on input over time, however, does not allow most language learners to reach a high level of academic language (VanPatten, 1996). Once students have reached a basic level of language proficiency, the use of grammar instruction should depend on the question, "What aspects of language are difficult for my students?" (Ellis, 2002). You will find that the areas of grammar that are challenging to students reflect their developmental level, their native language, and the presence or absence of particular structures in the L1.

Although traditional grammar instruction has focused on the memorization and application of grammar rules, there has been a shift toward stressing grammar points that focus on meaning (Ellis, 2002). Rather than simply explaining how a grammar structure functions, teachers encourage students to discover how language works, thereby increasing their linguistic analytical skills. For example, the *focus on form* approach relies on teachers and peers to direct a language learner's attention to a grammatical structure when they experience difficulty with it, either in oral or written language (Long & Robinson, 1998). The goal is not merely to correct them, but to explain how the structure is used and to provide meaningful examples. This type of grammar instruction is authentic and focused on students' needs, helping them develop understanding of both form and meaning. In the example below, instruction in grammar is purposeful and culminates with practical application to students' own writing.

TRY THIS!

Upper Elementary and Secondary Level

Intermediate and Advanced L2 Level

Some ELLs have difficulty with the *ed* ending in their writing. To focus their attention on how *ed* is used, ask them to go through a text you are already using in the class to identify where *ed* is used, and then explain why it's necessary. In other words, what meaning does it convey? Then students can go back to their own writing to edit for *ed* usage. Although this type of lesson will help clarify this aspect of language, students will need consistent and repeated reinforcement throughout the year.

As bilingual teachers, we are always teaching language, whether implicitly or explicitly. While content is often dictated by the curriculum, the explicit teaching of grammar should be driven by our students' needs. Though it's unnecessary to teach an area of language that students have already mastered, we need to support students as they heighten their understanding of how syntax works to make language comprehensible.

Tung, a fourth- and fifth-grade Chinese bilingual teacher, takes a balanced approach to teaching about the fluidity and versatility of language. He does not evade standard rules, but rather complements them with explanations about how rules can be broken in different contexts.

> I do teach grammar. . . . I tell them that you have to know the rules before you can break them. Otherwise, you don't know what you're doing. But I try not to use grammar textbooks; I use the pattern books. I do a lot of sentence patterns, and I make them draw charts and graphs and sentences, I do all those things.

Return to the Essential Question

Do I need to have a separate time slot for teaching English as a second language?

One Teacher's Response

In my district, for the first time, a separate time for teaching language only is being mandated. Some call it ELD, some ESOL, some ESL. It does not matter what you call it; it is the explicit teaching of the L2 for our bilingual students. There is huge disagreement over this action, even though it is a state mandate and we don't have a choice. At first I was against it. I thought that sheltering instruction was enough in some situations. But I have been going through a deep process of reflection, and now I think it is basically a good idea. I mean, basically . . . there are always exceptions. But our district is made up of almost 75% bilingual students. We can't just assume they will learn academic English without some focused attention to it. And that attention has to be different because they are coming to the classroom with different skills and experiences than, say, the English monolingual high school student who takes English as a requirement to graduate high school.

Charles, an administrator in a K–12 public school district, shares his reflections on the new ESL policy that is being implemented where he works. He has come to believe that, in most situations, a separate time slot for teaching the L2 is needed. Yet he recognizes that there is the need for exceptions to every policy. Although it is generally recognized that there is a need for explicit instruction in the L2, there is a range of opinion as well as a range of context that needs to be considered. Bilingual teachers need to balance state mandates with student needs. In the end, this is a question you will need to answer for yourself, and along with others in your school, based upon your own unique students and situation. Similarly, you will need to reflect upon the increasing role of federal and state-mandated assessments in the education of your emergent bilingual students. This will be the focus of the next chapter.

NOTE

1. ESL is also referred to as English for Speakers of Other Languages (ESOL), Teaching English to Speakers of Other Languages (TESOL), and English Language Development (ELD)

REFERENCES

Calderón, M. E. (2007). *Teaching reading to English language learners, grades 6–12: A framework for improving achievement in the content areas.* Thousand Oaks, CA: Corwin.

Crawford, J., & Krashen, S. (2007). *English learners in American classrooms: 101 questions 101 answers.* New York: Scholastic.

Ellis, R. (2002). The place of grammar instruction in the second/foreign language curriculum. In E. Hinkel and S. Fotos (Eds.), *New perspectives on grammar teaching in second language classrooms.* Mahwah, NJ: Lawrence Erlbaum.

Krashen, S. (1985). *The input hypothesis.* Harlow, UK: Longman.

Lewis, M. (1993). *The lexical approach.* Hove, UK: Language Teaching Publications.

Long, M., & Robinson, P. (1998). Focus on form: Theory, research, and practice. In C. Doughty & J. Williams (Eds.), *Focus on form in classroom second language acquisition* (pp. 15–63). Cambridge, MA: Cambridge University Press.

Menken, K., Kleyn, T., & Chae, N. (2007). *Meeting the needs of long-term English learners in high schools.* Report to the New York City Department of Education, Office of English Learners.

Multimedia Project (2000). Why do project-based learning? Redwood City, CA: The Multimedia Project. Retrieved December 30, 2008, from http://pblmm .k12.ca.us/PBLGuide/WhyPBL.html

Reyes, S. A., & Vallone, T. L. (2008). *Constructivist strategies for teaching English language learners.* Thousand Oaks, CA: Corwin.

VanPatten, B. (Ed.) (1996). *Input processing and grammar instruction in a second language: Theory and research.* Westport, CT: Greenwood.

Walqui, A., & van Lier, L. (2009). *Scaffolding the academic success of English language learners: A pedagogy of promise.* San Francisco: WestEd.

Wiesner, D. (1991). *Tuesday.* New York: Clarion Books.

7

Assessing Bilingual Students

Essential Question

How is assessment different in the bilingual classroom?

One Teacher's Dilemma

I'll be honest with you, like two months before the test we just rehearse them like mad and they get good results.

Although some districts are beginning to frown on the inordinate amount of time spent on preparation for standardized tests, educators still feel the pressure to get scores up. After all, who would want the sanctions that come with too many years of not making "adequate yearly progress" as specified by the No Child Left Behind (NCLB) Act. Chinese bilingual teacher Tung acknowledges that despite pressure to limit preparation for standardized tests to three hours per week, bilingual educators in his school push the limit to ensure better test scores. This is not surprising given that bilingual teachers have the unenviable task of preparing students to take high-stakes tests in their second language.

In the NCLB era, many educators are questioning a national overreliance on tests and asking whether standardized tests are fair for emergent bilingual students. *Assessment* has become synonymous with *standardized testing* in the minds of many educators. Yet there are many other issues involved in assessment for ELLs. This chapter not only discusses the implications of NCLB for bilingual instruction, but also provides examples of appropriate uses of assessment with these students.

LANGUAGE DOMINANCE AND PROFICIENCY

Rare is the bilingual (or multilingual) individual who is equally proficient in all languages spoken. Most of us are dominant in one language or another; it is unrealistic to expect otherwise. Thus, when students enter a bilingual program, it is essential that their language skills be assessed so that they receive appropriate educational services. This includes levels of L1 proficiency, levels of L2 proficiency, and a determination of language dominance. Students who are dominant in English, with either a high or a low level of L2 proficiency, should be placed in additive bilingual programs. Students with high L1 and low L2 proficiency levels can be well served in a variety of bilingual program models. Students who have low levels of proficiency in both of the tested languages need to be considered carefully. For example, a child from Mexico may be tested in Spanish and in English, but it is possible that the L1 is an indigenous language such as Mixteco. If no educational programs are available in Mixteco, multiple factors will have to be considered to ensure proper placement of the student. For example, how old is the student, and has his or her prior educational experience been in English or in Spanish? Do the parents speak Spanish at home? What do parents want and why? Should the student receive academic instruction in one new language or in two?

Formal instruments have been created to help educators determine the levels of L1 and L2 proficiency, as well as language dominance. A few of the more commonly used language proficiency assessments are described as follows:

- The Woodcock-Muñoz Language Survey–Revised (WMLS–R) assesses language proficiency in English and Spanish for pre-K through adult, and it can be used to determine eligibility for bilingual services.
- The Language Assessment Battery (LAB) measures Spanish language proficiency in speaking, listening, reading, and writing for Grades K–12, and it is used for determining the language of dominance and for evaluating programs in schools that have a substantial proportion of Spanish-speaking students.

- The Language Assessment Scales—English for Reading and Writing (LAS R/W) is a battery of reading and writing competency tests for Grades 2–12. It is intended for use in placing and reclassifying ELLs. The LAS R/W may be used alone or in combination with the LAS-Oral to provide a complete picture of language competency.
- The Language Assessment Scales-Oral (LAS-O) is available in English and Spanish and is used to test proficiency in speaking and listening for ELLs in Grades 1–12. The LAS-O in English measures the oral language skills necessary to succeed in a mainstream American academic environment for Grades 1–12.
- The Foreign Language Assessment Directory (FLAD) is a free, searchable database with information on more than 200 assessments in over 90 languages other than English. FLAD contains information about assessments that are currently used in elementary, middle, secondary, and post-secondary school programs around the United States. It is provided as a free service of the Center for Applied Linguistics (CAL) and can be assessed at the following Web site: http://www.cal.org/CalWebDB/FLAD/

ACADEMIC ACHIEVEMENT IN THE L1

There are essentially two ways to assess student academic achievement in the native language. The most natural approach is to use an authentic assessment, which is also consistent with constructivist, critical, and culturally responsive pedagogy. Subsequent sections in this chapter will give more specific information on the use of authentic assessments. Another approach is to use formal tests that have been created and normed by specific publishers. Of course, a plethora of academic achievement tests exist for use with English-dominant students, or students with high levels of English language proficiency.

A number of similar tests exist in Spanish, although few are available in other languages. States determine what will be accepted as evidence of student learning in a language other than English. Information should be made available through your state's educational department. Two of the most commonly used instruments to assess student academic achievement in Spanish are *Aprenda* and *La Prueba de Realizacion*. *Aprenda: La prueba de logros en español, Tercera edición (Aprenda 3)*, originally published by the California Department of Education, was developed for use with K–12 Spanish-dominant students to measure academic achievement in the L1. It was modeled after the Stanford Achievement Test Series, Tenth Edition (Stanford 10), as its Spanish-language equivalent. *La Prueba de Realizacion* (1997) is also an academic achievement test in Spanish for K–12 students, developed to measure both Spanish literacy and Spanish content area achievement. *Logramos*, Second Edition, (2006), published by Riverside, is also a K–12, comprehensive assessment of student progress in the basic skills in Spanish.

Even if academic achievement tests are not required in the L1, some schools and districts choose to use them in order to have a more accurate assessment of the academic achievement of bilingual students. Remember, these are *not* tests of language proficiency, but of student learning in content areas.

ASSESSMENT OF ACCULTURATION

It is not unusual for adolescent immigrant students to be referred for evaluation for exceptionalities due to symptoms such as "anxiety, reluctance to attend school, truancy, withdrawal from usual activities and friends, low self-confidence, and a sense of hopelessness" (Reyes & Dinkha, 2005, p. 18). Yet such symptoms can also reflect problems of acculturation that occur when an individual "who is already socialized to a particular set of norms comes into contact with those of another culture, where norms or ways may be markedly different" (Herrera, Murry, & Morales Cabral, 2007, p. 81).

Acculturation can be a traumatic process, compounded by events such as war, chaotic departure, and separation from important family members. It is easy to imagine how such difficulties can impact student learning and achievement. (Disengagement, behavioral issues, and social maladjustment may mimic some symptoms of disability. However, if these are instead symptoms of a traumatic acculturation, this should become apparent in the preassessment process.) Acculturation is also related to identity, which may impact not only psychosocial well-being, but linguistic and academic achievement as well (Reyes & Dinkha, 2005). Therefore, before a decision is made to refer a student, it is absolutely essential that an assessment of acculturation be done. Even in the event that referral is not a consideration, an acculturation assessment can reveal information relevant to program placement as well as classroom instruction and socialization. Most acculturation instruments examine the amount of time spent in the school or school district, the amount of time spent in bilingual or ESL programs, the levels of proficiency in both the L1 and the L2, the cultural background (ethnicity and national origin), and the percentage of students in the school who speak the same language or dialect as that of the new arrival (Herrera et al., 2007).

Acculturation, as with language proficiency and academic achievement, can be measured by both authentic and formal means. Herrera et al. (2007) recommend the use of the Acculturation Quick Screen (AQS). However, your school or districts' student entry survey can easily be adapted to include the information noted above. In addition, there are many classroom activities in which you can involve all of your students that are both enjoyable and revealing in terms of important acculturation information.

Teachers should be aware that acculturation is a significant consideration in the bilingual classroom and should be sensitive to its manifestations, which can include assimilation or accommodation. Contrary to dominant-culture rhetoric, assimilation is not necessarily a positive outcome. Assimilation implies the replacement of native language, culture, beliefs and values (deep culture), and behavioral norms with those of the new culture. In this sense, it can be considered subtractive in nature. Accommodation, by contrast, is additive. Heritage is securely practiced and maintained, but the ability to understand and fully function across new cultures is developed and sustained. Accommodation may also foster the development of hybrid practices that blend the new and the old. But acculturation sometimes poses challenges that teachers are not professionally prepared to address (particularly in adolescence, when identity issues typically come to the fore). In these situations, teachers should seek the assistance of school counselors and other professional staff that can either guide them in this area or work with individual students to support them as they adapt to life in a new culture.

TRY THIS!

Varied Grade Levels (See Each Activity)

The following activities were designed for use with bilingual immigrant students, but they could easily be adapted for multiple purposes and student populations:

- Have each student draw or write (in the L1) about one of her or his most important life events in the country of origin. Repeat this activity, but this time focus on contemporary life in the United States. (Upper Elementary Level)

(Continued)

(Continued)

- Use structured poetry in the L1 on topics that address identity construction. For example, use haikus on the topic of the self ("me") or on the topic of being bilingual or bicultural. (Lower Elementary Level)
- Have a collection of literature at the appropriate L1 reading level in the class that focuses on the immigration experience. Have the students keep a journal about the protagonist in which they compare and contrast the experience of the protagonist with their own experiences. (Secondary Level)
- Have the class create a mural on the immigration experience. Post the mural on a prominent wall in your classroom. (Upper Elementary Level)

Figure 7.1 shows another way to use the structured poetry approach. In Elizabeth's fifth-grade, two-way bilingual immersion class, students were asked to write a bilingual poem that started with their first names, ended with their last names, and listed three adjectives to describe themselves in between. They completed English stems (such as "brother of," "I am from," and "who loves") with Spanish endings.

Figure 7.1

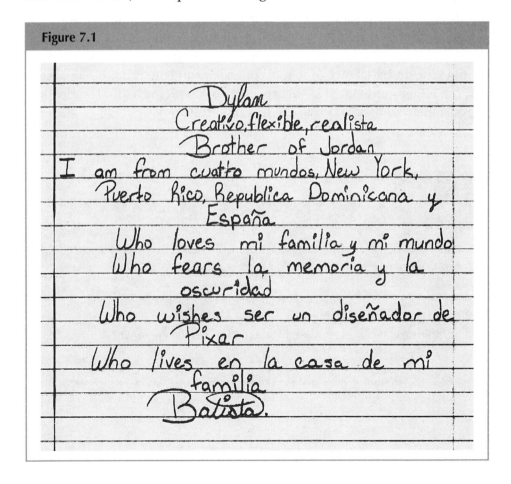

English Translation:

Dylan

Creative, Flexible, Realist

I am from four worlds, New York, Puerto Rico,
Dominican Republic and Spain

Who loves my family and my world

Who fears memories and the dark

Who wishes to be a designer for Pixar

Who lives in the house of my family

Batista

Source: Created by Dylan Batista. Used with permission.

This type of poetry writing allows students to reflect upon different aspects of their identity, including being bilingual, because they are free to use all the languages that fall within their linguistic repertoire. As with previously suggested immigration activities, the resulting student artifacts can provide educators with valuable information on how students are negotiating the acculturation process.

TO REFER OR NOT TO REFER FOR SPECIAL SERVICES, THAT IS THE QUESTION!

A long, sad history of disproportionate ELL placements in special education continues into the present (Collier, 2008). So the question of whether or not to refer a bilingual student who may or may not have an exceptionality is crucial. The unfortunate tradition of inappropriate referrals and placements is compounded by confusion between characteristics of ELLs and characteristics of students with exceptionalities.

As previously noted, acculturation difficulties can be a source of such confusion. So can linguistic and cultural differences. Bilingual education and special education are distinct fields, and simply combining the two does not make one an expert in assessing and working with bilingual students with exceptionalities. All of these factors serve to complicate the educator's dilemma in determining whether or not to refer an ELL for special education services. The good news for bilingual teachers is that, while you are responsible for preassessment of ELLs, you are not responsible for their actual assessment; that is the job of a qualified professional. Furthermore, you probably know much more than you think you do. For example, you should be able to determine whether a learning difficulty exists in the L2, though not in the

L1, and whether the student is having difficulties in second language development when appropriate modifications are in place. Through collecting data that is available within the school, and through interviews with parents or other appropriate family members, you should be able to determine whether the student in question received appropriate native and second language instruction in the past and whether other educators who interact with the student in the current context are qualified to work with ELLs. All of this places you in an excellent position to think intelligently about whether or not a student is responding normally to environmental factors.

If you suspect that the learning difficulty a student is experiencing is not due to normal contextual experiences, it is time to think about pre-referral. Collier (2005) suggests a thorough examination of prior schooling, home language, English proficiency, academic achievement, student behavior, and adaptation in the acculturation process before a special education referral takes place. Herrera et al. (2007) provide a pre-referral flowchart that succinctly summarizes what teachers should know before referring a culturally and linguistically diverse (CLD) student for special education services. They suggest that the first step in the pre-referral process is quite simply to determine whether the student is experiencing atypical learning problems. (Our reminder would be that the atypical learning problems should be in comparison to other ELLs and that they occur in both languages.) If not, the process should immediately end. If so, the next element to examine is attendance, mobility, and medical and psychological issues. After obtaining the appropriate records and applying any needed intervention, reassess after sufficient time has elapsed. If the learning problem persists, next check to see if the student's educational program has been aligned with the student's specific linguistic, academic, and social needs. Assess student learning under varied classroom conditions using varied instructional approaches. If the result is negative at either point, changes or accommodations need to be made. If, after sufficient time with these modifications, academic difficulties persist, it is time to consider referral.

Response to Intervention (RTI) is gaining attention as an approach to serving students who are struggling academically. In this model, educators use instructional interventions that gradually increase in levels of intensity that are referred to as *tiers*. Each tier includes accompanying assessments that lead to a decision: the student needs additional instruction, the student needs additional intervention in general education, or the student needs referral to special education. Collier (2008) applies this model to second language contexts. She notes that for ELLs "specific areas that need to be screened and monitored during the Tier 2 and Tier 3 process . . . include: acculturation and level of culture shock, prior experience, cognitive learning style, background in culture and language, and level of language acquisition" (p. 95).

We recommend that every ELL (referred to by Herrera et al. [2007] as *CLD*) who enters a school or educational system should go through a thorough process to ensure correct program and instructional placement from the start. Early attention to linguistic and cultural difference and to immigration history can often avoid the pre-referral process altogether. Part of the solution to the problem of overrepresentation of ELLs in special education begins in the educational placement process. Another part of the solution lies in the professional knowledge and skills of the bilingual classroom teacher.

USING AUTHENTIC ASSESSMENTS WITHIN A CLIMATE OF STANDARDIZED TESTING

In the best case scenario, assessment should occur over time to inform teachers of students' learning and how to modify their instruction (Gottlieb, 2006). There are many ways to assess students, although the most common form has become the test. Standardized exams, as well as classroom tests, typically ask decontextualized questions. Conversely, an authentic assessment allows teachers to evaluate students' learning through real-world types of tasks and projects that often require the application and synthesis of concepts. Authentic assessments thus allow greater opportunities for the higher levels of Bloom's taxonomy, rather than the constricting "right or wrong" approach of tests. Another weakness of standardized tests is that they are meant to evaluate a student's content understanding, yet for ELLs they are first and foremost a language test (García & Menken, 2006). As a result, second language learners may not be able to show their full competency when an exam is in their nondominant language. Authentic assessments, by contrast, allow students to use language in a more contextualized way to show understanding through a variety of formats, such as visuals, drama, or presentations.

Let's imagine an assessment scenario. If we were teaching you how to do a handstand, we could assess you by providing a multiple-choice test with questions about the kick-up stance, the positioning of your hands, and the alignment of your body. This would show us whether you know the basics. However, we can only verify that you can *apply* this knowledge through a more authentic type of assessment. This might include having you do a handstand or having you explain the steps as you go through the process of doing the handstand. We could then ask you to reflect on your efforts to see where you could have improved. The latter process provides a more realistic assessment that checks for understanding, application, and evaluation at a variety of levels. Authentic assessment is closely tied to what actually occurs in the classroom, while wide scale assessments are often disconnected from classroom life. In the classroom, examples of authentic assessments range from designing scientific experiments, to building a structure using one's knowledge of geometrical concepts, to debating two (or more) sides of undocumented immigration in the United States.

Portfolios are another example of how to authentically assess students in a comprehensive way that allows them to present and reflect upon their work and growth in a given subject area. This type of assessment also allows students to showcase and reflect on their growth in one or both languages (O'Malley & Valdez Pierce, 1996). Portfolios generally include work samples selected by students. This may include a reflection questionnaire or a brief write-up on each artifact that summarizes the piece, describes what the student learned, and identifies areas for future improvement. Upon completion, students can present their portfolio to families, peers, teachers, and administrators in a formal setting. These events position students as experts as they describe their content learning and processes and even take questions from audience members. Once you have instituted portfolios as an assessment tool, you can invite students from prior years to present their portfolios as a model and to answer questions that current students may have about the process.

While hard-copy portfolios are certainly acceptable, students can also create electronic portfolios through specialized software programs, or they can even use more common programs such as PowerPoint or Keynote where they can scan in their work, upload photographs or video clips, and create a succinct slideshow for presentation. In a bilingual classroom, the language of the portfolio must be negotiated as you consider the content of the portfolio and the language(s) of instruction related to the topic. Therefore, a portfolio can be bilingual, in the LOTE, or in English, but this decision must be made purposefully at the onset.

TRY THIS!

Elementary and Secondary Level

Before embarking on a unit of study, decide on the criteria to assess students through the creation of a portfolio. Consider the following areas as you plan, either individually or preferably with other content or grade-level teachers:

- Whether the portfolio will cover one area or will be interdisciplinary
- The range of entries or artifacts required for the portfolio
- The type of entries acceptable for the portfolio (e.g., essays, photographs, diagrams, letters, or short video clips)

- The type of reflection students will complete for each entry or for the portfolio as a whole
- The language(s) of the portfolio
- The medium of the portfolio (i.e., hard copy, electronic, or both)
- A rubric to assess all parts of the portfolio (e.g., connections to content, conceptual learning, depth of reflections, writing, and language growth)
- How and to whom students will present their portfolios

Although portfolios have become relatively common, the danger is that they turn into nothing more than a folder of mandated assignments, rather than a collection of work students select that showcases their progress and learning over time. Therefore, while the teacher, in collaboration with students, should set the general guidelines, the final decisions should be made by the student.

The use of authentic assessments requires careful evaluation. While tests are clear-cut, often graded by point value or percentage per question, authentic assessments can be evaluated via rubrics designed with a variety of criteria in mind. A rubric can include categories related to the process, content learning, outcomes, and language use. Furthermore, students can evaluate their own work, and that of their peers, once they are taught how to do so in a thoughtful manner. Figure 7.2 is an example of a rubric used to assess a poetry anthology that connected the genre of poetry with the topic of identity. Because poetry is a genre that allows for considerable grammatical liberty, the evaluative focus was on content, vocabulary, and overall process. In other genres, you may also want to include a section on language mechanics. The rubric may be used in different ways: it can serve as a formative assessment for students and teachers to see where they are in the process and how they can improve, or it can be used as a summative assessment at the completion of the unit when a grade is given. To calculate the final grade in Figure 7.2, simply divide the total number of points possible, 28, by the number of points earned.

While assessing students through authentic tasks and projects takes a great deal of thought and planning, it is important to include this type of assessment in your practice. Authentic assessment that occurs over time allows teachers to better understand which aspects of content and language the students have mastered and where they need additional support.

Tests have a place in teaching and learning, but they provide only limited ways for students to demonstrate their understanding, application, and synthesis of complex concepts at one point in time. Test results can

Figure 7.2

	4—Exceptional	3—Proficient	2—Developing	1—Beginning
Content	Student has written more than 5 poems. They may include <ul><li>1 identity poem</li><li>1 family poem</li><li>1 culture experience poem</li><li>1 object poem</li><li>2 or more poems of his or her choice</li></ul>	Student has written 5 poems. They may include <ul><li>1 identity poem</li><li>1 family poem</li><li>1 culture experience poem</li><li>1 object poem</li><li>1 poem of his or her choice</li></ul>	Student has written 3 or 4 poems. They may include <ul><li>1 identity poem</li><li>1 family poem</li><li>1 culture experience poem</li><li>1 object poem</li><li>2 poems of his or her choice</li></ul>	Student has written 1 or 2 poems. They may include <ul><li>1 identity poem</li><li>1 family poem</li><li>1 culture experience poem</li><li>1 object poem</li><li>1 poem of his or her choice</li></ul>
	Poems have many poetic elements, including metaphors and similes	Poems have some poetic elements, including metaphors and similes	Student attempts to use poetic elements, including metaphors and similes	Poems do not have any poetic elements, including metaphors and similes
	Poems include many concrete and sensory images	Poems include some concrete and sensory images	Student attempts to include concrete and sensory images	Poems do not include any concrete and sensory images
	Student's identity is clearly reflected throughout all poems	Student's identity is clearly reflected in most poems	Student attempts to reflect identity through poems	Student's identity is not reflected through poems
Word Choice	Many interesting vocabulary words used	Some interesting vocabulary words used	A few interesting vocabulary words used	No interesting vocabulary words used

	4—Exceptional	3—Proficient	2—Developing	1—Beginning
Process	All steps of the writing process are turned in: draft, revisions, and final copy	Most steps of the writing process are turned in: draft, revisions, and final copy	Some steps of the writing process are missing	Few steps of the writing process were followed
	Student edited paper independently and with partner	Student edited paper with help from teacher	Student relied on teacher to edit work	Student did little or no editing

Created by Elizabeth Silva, Surky Mateo, Jaqueline Rodríguez, and Wenn Siak

also be distorted by extraneous factors unrelated to children's learning. Students may feel ill, hungry, be in a bad mood, not care about the test, or even try to fail it on purpose (as with some students who prefer to continue receiving ELL services). Moreover, once students enter the "real world," it is unlikely they will be required to show what they know through isolated questions and answers. Instead, they will have to produce reports, use their creativity to come up with solutions, or design plans. Authentic assessment not only seeks to mirror the skills required in society, but also creates a more meaningful way of learning than a curriculum organized around standardized tests.

NEGOTIATING STANDARDS WHILE MEETING THE NEEDS OF STUDENTS

Rosario's classroom walls were adorned with student essays that explained how their first names were conceived of; graphic organizers that webbed aspects of a community; flags from the United States, Puerto Rico, and Mexico; and maps of the world, North America, and the United States. Right next to the door, a different type of chart was hung to remind students of upcoming events in February:

Special Days in February
Picture Day
President's Week
Citywide Reading Test
Spanish Test
Citywide Math Test
NYSESLAT (New York State English as a Second Language Achievement Test)

In a time when standardized testing has become a feature of education that we cannot escape—as evidenced in the "special days" posted for Rosario's fifth-grade class—we must constantly remind ourselves that there are other ways to assess students that are meaningful, authentic, and reflective of their cultural and linguistic backgrounds (Gay, 2000; Neill et al., 1995). The imposition of state standards and standardized exams has the potential to dictate classroom content without considering student needs.

Thus, teachers today must perform a balancing act. Although they must address state standards in their instruction, they can choose to begin from the standards or from the needs of their students. Sleeter (2005) describes a standards-conscious approach toward curriculum planning in which "standards are a tool, but not the starting point, and do not define the central organizing ideas and ideology of one's curriculum" (p. 60). Thus, testing becomes less important than the way curriculum and instruction are designed.

Let's see how this approach might look. The following are California's science standards related to climate at the secondary level:

Climate is the long-term average of a region's weather and depends on many factors.

As a basis for understanding this concept:

a. *Students know* weather (in the short run) and climate (in the long run) involve the transfer of energy into and out of the atmosphere.

b. *Students know* the effects on climate of latitude, elevation, topography, and proximity to large bodies of water and cold or warm ocean currents.

c. *Students know* how Earth's climate has changed over time, corresponding to changes in Earth's geography, atmospheric composition, and other factors, such as solar radiation and plate movement.

    d. *Students know* how computer models are used to predict the effects of the increase in greenhouse gases on climate for the planet as a whole and for specific regions. (California Department of Education, 2003, p. 50)

Rather than starting from the standards and exploring them in general, students could be asked to consider local, national, and global events that have had a great impact on our planet. Whether they are interested in exploring the air quality in the Bay Area, Hurricane Katrina (which would also bring in social studies standards), or the tsunami in Southeast Asia, the above standards can be applied to any of these phenomena. In this way, the curriculum depends on the student, teacher, and local realities and curiosities. But it connects to the standards, rather than allowing the standards to dictate content without regard to the cultural backgrounds and interests of the students.

NEGOTIATING THE LANGUAGE(S) OF STANDARDIZED TESTS

Requirements for high-stakes testing have a major impact on bilingual classrooms, often overriding program designs and imposing a de facto language policy. In a study of ten New York City high schools, Menken (2008) found that nine schools changed their language of instruction to English in order to be consistent with the language of the test. One school, however, increased instruction in the LOTE by requiring students to take Advanced Placement (AP) Spanish. As a result, both test scores in Spanish and test scores in English Language Arts improved significantly. Educators at this school understood that the concepts and skills required in both Spanish and English Language Arts were similar, and would transfer from Spanish (the L1) to English (the L2). This suggests that language of instruction decisions based on what is best for students can also result in better test scores.

    Currently, a handful of states, such as New York, Texas, and New Mexico, provide test translations in a few languages in the core content areas (other than in English Language Arts). Since testing policies change, it is recommended that you inquire into the native language assessments available in your state. While students usually take the test in either English or their LOTE, the teachers in at least one Haitian Creole bilingual program test their students in both languages. This strategy uses students' bilingualism as a strength and taps that knowledge to assess the content and language in a more holistic manner (Shohamy, 2001; Valdes & Figueroa, 1994).

Most assessments that have the highest stakes attached are in English (Rivera & Collum, 2006). Dina, a Russian component dual language teacher, faces a different situation. She explains, "We don't have any formal Russian assessments, which isn't really a good thing because I have to create my own, so that's more work." On the one hand, the lack of assessments allows Dina more freedom to teach the skills and content that she feels her students need the most. On the other hand, the lack of assessments in Russian implicitly devalues the language and content taught in that language for parents and the school administration. Bilingual teachers in this situation need to stress to families the importance of the LOTE. This can be done in part by providing authentic assessments, tests, and report card grades in the native language(s) of the students.

Return to the Essential Question

How is assessment different in the bilingual classroom?

One Teacher's Response

I came back to the first-grade teachers and I said we've got to do something. As much as I hate the testing, we've got to give them those skills, and we can't wait until second or third grade. We've got to start now, so let's have a discussion about how we can start implementing some of those skills now, because you know what? They can do it. If we really model it well they'll be able to pick it up and they'll become more sophisticated, I hope, as the years go by. So we invited the fourth-grade teacher so we're going to be looking at the ELA (English Language Assessment) and look at what skills they need.

Araceli, a Spanish bilingual teacher, understands that we cannot live outside our culture. Unfortunately, in the United States today, that means an educational culture focused on standardized, high-stakes assessments. We suggest a three-point strategy for living within a culture in which we do not necessarily agree. First, whenever possible, use authentic measures of assessment that are a natural part of the instructional process. Second, give our students the skills they need to do well on assessments while instilling a spirit of critique. Third, become an advocate for your students and their families, a theme we will discuss in Chapter 9. Before doing so, however, we will hear from some experienced bilingual educators as they reflect upon concepts we have discussed thus far.

REFERENCES

California Department of Education. (2003). *Science content standards for California public schools: Kindergarten through grade twelve.* CA: Author.

Collier, C. (2005). Separating language difference from disability. *NABE News, 28.3,* 13–17.

Collier, C. (2008). *Separating difference from disability.* Ferndale, WA: CrossCultural Developmental Education Service.

García, O., & Menken, K. (2006). The English of Latinos from a plurilingual transcultural angle: Implication for assessment and schools. In S. Nero (Ed.), *Dialects, Englishes, Creoles and education.* Clevedon: Multilingual Matters.

Gay, G. (2000). *Culturally responsive teaching: Theory, research, and practice.* New York: Teachers College Press.

Gottlieb, M. (2006). *Assessing English language learners: Bridges from language proficiency to academic proficiency.* Thousand Oaks, CA: Corwin.

Herrera, S. G., Murry, K. G., & Morales Cabral, R. (2007). *Assessment accommodations for classroom teachers of culturally and linguistically diverse students.* New York: Pearson.

Menken, K. (2008). *English learners left behind: Standardized testing as language policy.* Clevedon, UK: Multilingual Matters.

Neill, M., Bursh, P., Schaeffer, B., Thall, C., Yohe, M., & Zappardino, P. (1995). *Implementing performance assessments.* Cambridge, MA: FairTest.

O'Malley, J. M., & Valdez Pierce, L. (1996). *Authentic assessment for English language learners: Practical approaches for teachers.* New York: Addison-Wesley.

Reyes, S. A., & Dinkha, J. (2005). Psychological well-being of adolescent immigrant students: Recommendations for school practice. *NABE News, 28.3,* 8–21.

Rivera, C., & Collum, E. (Eds.). (2006). *State assessment policy and practice for English language learners: A national perspective.* Mahwah, NJ: Lawrence Erlbaum.

Shohamy, E. (2001). *The power of tests: A critical perspective of the uses of language tests.* New York: Longman.

Sleeter, C. E. (2005). *Un-standardizing curriculum: Multicultural teaching in the standards-based classroom.* New York: Teachers College Press.

Valdes, G., & Figueroa, R. A. (1994). *Bilingualism and testing: A special case of bias.* Norwood, NJ: Ablex.

REFERENCES FOR CITED ASSESSMENTS

Aprenda: La prueba de logros en español, Tercera edición (Aprenda 3). (1997). San Antonio, Texas: Pearson.

La Prueba de Realizacion. (1991). Rolling Meadows, IL: Riverside Publishing.

Language Assessment Battery (LAB). (1982). New York: New York City Board of Education.

Language Assessment Scales (LAS). (1990). Monterey, CA: CTB/McGraw-Hill.

Language Assessment Scales-Oral. (LAS-O). (1990). Monterey, CA: CTB/McGraw-Hill.

Logramos, Second edition. (2006). Rolling Meadows, IL: Riverside.

Woodcock-Muñoz Language Survey–Revised (WMLS-R). (1993). Rolling Meadows, IL: Riverside.

8

Expanding the Bilingual Context

Essential Question

How can bilingual curriculum and instruction be applied to multiple learning contexts?

In this chapter, we use a different format to broaden the context of programs that fall under the umbrella of bilingual education or that contribute to students' bilingualism. We go beyond the more common transitional and maintenance bilingual programs to highlight other models that make up the field. (Definitions of each model can be found in Chapter 1.) In order to gain an in-depth understanding of the various program models, we asked exemplary educators in each of these areas to describe their specific model, its related challenges, and how they work to overcome those challenges. We have also asked them to include any suggestions they might have for future and beginning teachers who will work within that specific model. After each teacher's response, we follow up by reviewing the key areas that were discussed across the chapters of this book that are especially relevant for teachers in each program type.

TWO-WAY BILINGUAL IMMERSION

Katherine Baldwin, two-way bilingual immersion teacher
for P.S. 75—The Emily Dickenson School—in New York, NY

Program Description

The dual language program that I work in at P.S. 75 is truly unique for many reasons, but mainly because it emphasizes that all students should maintain their native home language while learning a second language at school. About half of the students in our program speak Spanish at home and are learning to read and write in both Spanish and English at school. The other half of the students speak English at home and are also learning to read and write in both Spanish and English at school. We also frequently work with students who speak a different language at home—like Portuguese, Italian, or Mixteco, to name a few. These students are then learning in their second and third languages. Unlike many bilingual programs that transition students to English without maintaining their native language, our program gives equal instructional time to both languages, and we expect that our fifth graders will leave the program equally proficient in English and Spanish. Our program also allows for classrooms with a wealth of children and families from all over the world, which creates cross-cultural experiences that may not exist in other programs.

Facing and Overcoming Challenges

Especially in the early grades, learning a new language is a difficult task for many students. English-speaking students in the first grade will often stare blankly at their teacher when it is a Spanish day and a lesson is taught in their second language. So the teachers in the program have to use a lot of visual cues and strategies, such as total physical response (TPR), to help engage students when they are learning in their second language. I have faced students who resisted the second language and turned off when instruction was not in their native language. Getting to know the students well—what they like a lot and what can hook them— is often a way to engage them even when instruction is not in their first language.

Another challenge we face comes from the fact that our program is incredibly diverse in all senses of the word: racially, linguistically, socioeconomically, culturally, and so on. I have students who have traveled extensively with their parents and have summer homes in other countries, and I have some students who barely leave their own neighborhood. The disparity between experiences and knowledge that different students come into the classroom with is huge, and it is often difficult to teach one lesson to such a diverse group of children. In my classroom, I try to create lessons that allow students to learn from one another and that are more open-ended and can be approached from different angles. This diversity leads to some amazing classroom discussions, but it is definitely difficult to plan for!

Recommendations for Teachers

Be patient as students learn their second language. Kids acquire language at different rates, and you can't expect that they will all learn with the same speed. Be sensitive to the fact that learning a second language is a very vulnerable experience. Your students are putting themselves out there and taking risks every time they speak or write a sentence in a language that they are still making sense of. Show them that you, too, are always learning and that even teachers make mistakes . . . and it's OK.

Adaptations for Teaching in a Two-Way Bilingual Immersion Classroom

- Often, though not always, two-way programs have more diverse classrooms. Build on this valuable resource by creating situations for students from different groups to work collaboratively and learn about one another.
- Create partnerships between families of different backgrounds so that students can continue to build friendships outside of school and parents can develop a network where they can get support when they have difficulty understanding their children's assignments in the second language.
- Shelter and scaffold language in both the L1 and the L2 because your students will come from a mix of English-dominant and LOTE-dominant backgrounds. Although it is unusual, sometimes you may have students for whom both English and the target language (LOTE) are second languages.
- Integrate language, content, and process in your instruction.

ONE-WAY DEVELOPMENTAL BILINGUAL EDUCATION

Josie Freeman (English component) and Rebeca Madrigal (Spanish component), partner teachers for P.S. 165—Robert E. Simon School—in New York, NY

Program Description

Our bilingual program was founded 16 years ago, and it continues to evolve, grow, and become a solid program. The program has historically been primarily for Spanish-language minority students. We also have students who speak Mixteco as their native language (an indigenous Mexican language) and are becoming trilingual as a result of our program. All of the bilingual teachers are sensitive to the linguistic needs of this population. The following are some of the elements that make this program successful and unique:

Team teaching. In first through fifth grade, teachers work in collaboration with a partner. There are two sets of students, and while the Spanish component teacher is working with group A in one classroom, the English component teacher is working with group B in another classroom. This structure allows teachers to collaborate and plan continuously during lunch, preparation time, and before and after school. The teams plan units, lessons, activities, and celebrations together so the two groups understand that they form a big group guided by two teachers who model a specific language. Lessons are planned to build up concepts and to reinforce them instead of repeating the same lesson.

Dual Language Study Group. Classroom teachers volunteer to participate in and facilitate a study group that focuses on issues specific to bilingual education. Teachers meet twice a month before school to discuss current issues, professional books, and concerns about the program, and to plan assemblies and retreats. The study group is the only avenue in which bilingual teachers can meet to have vertical conversations (across grades and with the same language component). This group enhances collaboration among teachers and partnerships. Its members become one voice to advocate for the needs of the students, families, and the program. The meetings help to revitalize the main mission of the program by reflecting on teacher practice, teaching philosophies, and theories.

Facing and Overcoming Challenges

There are a few challenges we face in our program. For the Spanish component, a huge challenge is the availability of good materials in Spanish, especially in the upper grades. Often books are translated poorly and are not accessible linguistically to our children. It is also difficult to acquire authentic literature for children in Spanish. Our teachers overcome this by doing their own translations of texts they want to use and by purchasing any materials they can when visiting Spanish-speaking countries. Professional development is also a concern because most of it occurs in English. Therefore, the Spanish-component teachers need to work together to develop a common language and terminology in order for the students to have access to such knowledge. For the English component, one of the big challenges in the lower grades is that we do not have strong English models.

Overall, we also need administrators who believe in the program and who would advocate for it on the district and regional level. We need highly qualified bilingual leaders to promote the program both in-house (to families, visitors, and new teachers) and outside of the program (to superintendents, universities, administrators, and political stakeholders). School administrators should make accommodations for bilingual teachers to have extra time to assess both groups. Bilingual teachers should be acknowledged for giving up their personal time to accommodate all of the families for parent-teacher conferences (in our case, 50 families). Finally, families should be more informed about the goals and the commitment to the bilingual program before they decide to enroll their child. Some families decide to take their child out of the program when she or he finishes the second grade. Parents get very concerned about the English and math exams, and they think that learning Spanish is taking away from learning English. Not all of the families believe that learning their native language is an asset to their academic and personal growth.

Recommendations for Teachers

A new teacher should know that collaboration is key in any school. In a bilingual program, collaboration becomes especially important because teachers should be concerned not only about their grade level, but about how their practice impacts the whole program as well. When it comes to co-teaching, it is important to form good partnerships. In a side-by-side model, both sides must be dedicated to planning together so that there is consistency of instruction for the children. Observing and talking with one another can reinforce this. Take note of classroom structures, routines, and even the way you speak to the children. Also, you must be clearly organized; otherwise, having two classes of children using your room every day can be overwhelming. You also want children to be able to access their own materials in both components without confusion. Therefore, streamline your labeling system so they know how to find things in both rooms. This can help develop consistency across the two components so that students feel equally comfortable in both classroom settings.

Adaptations for Teaching in a One-Way Developmental Bilingual Education Classroom

- Since students are likely to come from similar ethnic groups, ensure that you bring in a wide variety of resources, including books written by authors from different groups, videos, and guest speakers that expose students to diverse backgrounds and perspectives. This is especially important because our schools have become increasingly segregated.
- Provide classes for parents to learn English as well as literacy in the LOTE. This way, they can better help their children with schoolwork as they develop their own linguistic proficiencies.
- Shelter and scaffold language in the L2, but be aware of any students who may also need additional support in the L1.
- Integrate language, content, and process in your instruction.

ENGLISH AS A SECOND LANGUAGE (ESL)

Nelson Flores, former high school ESL teacher in New York, NY

Program Description

Our program is unique in that, rather than having separate ESL and content area classes, we assign a content teacher and an ESL teacher to team-teach. This allows both teachers to share their expertise with each other for the benefit of ELLs, with the content teacher able to contribute content knowledge and the ESL teacher able to contribute second-language-acquisition expertise and scaffolding strategies that many content teachers do not possess. They then carry out the lesson together, dividing up the work of presentation and implementation. Both teachers interact with all of the students in the class, and both are treated as the teachers of the class. This allows for more inclusion of ELLs in the general school environment, avoids stigmatizing them, and gives them the opportunity to socialize with and learn from native-English-speaking peers. In addition, as any teacher knows, having two pairs of eyes in the classroom is always a plus in terms of both classroom management and allowing for the flexibility to work with struggling students.

Facing and Overcoming Challenges

The challenge we face is that, in a content area class that is structured around content, it is sometimes difficult to plan for language. Team teaching provides many opportunities for scaffolding content, but this can quickly overtake the focus on language development. In addition, team teaching is very challenging for beginning students who have not yet mastered basic oral communication. We attempt to overcome these issues in the following ways:

- Trying to unpack the language and literacy needs of each content area and attempting to explicitly teach these ways of speaking and reading in an attempt to bring language back into the classroom explicitly, without losing the content (e.g., How would a historian say that, or what words would a historian use to write that?)
- Giving beginning students small-group instruction for a period of the day to work on these basic oral skills, allowing them to do their work in the content classes in their native language, and providing them with resources in their native language where necessary and appropriate

Recommendations for Teachers

I would advise any teachers working in a similar model to make sure they establish both of their roles in the classroom from the beginning. It is not beneficial for anybody involved for the content teacher to lead everything and the ESL teacher to be treated as a paraprofessional. Not only is this a waste of the resources that the ESL teacher offers, but it also sends a message to students that the ESL teacher is not a real teacher who is worthy of their respect. Setting procedures and dividing up the work of every lesson is the only way to prevent this from happening. In addition, it is important for both teachers to set time to plan together and to work from their strengths. The content teacher should be working on the content objectives and the ESL teacher should be working on the scaffolding of the content as well as the language objectives. While there may be some overlap, there is no need for both teachers to sit down together to plan every lesson. The content teacher can draft a lesson based on content objectives and then send it to the ESL teacher for modifications and the addition of language objectives.

Adaptations for Teaching ESL

- If your classroom has a diverse cultural and linguistic student body, bring in a family member to share his or her language and culture. This can provide a great opportunity for students to develop language awareness as they see the similarities and differences across languages and cultures (Hélot & Young, 2006).
- When reading books with the class, allow students to use translated versions to either read in class or at home.
- Allow students who speak the same native language to discuss the content of lessons in their L1 before doing the work in English. This will allow them to clarify directions, answer questions, and deepen conceptual understandings—which will transfer into English.
- Shelter and scaffold language in the L2.
- Integrate language, content, and process in your instruction.

TEACHING BILINGUAL STUDENTS WITH EXCEPTIONALITIES

Elizabeth Silva, fifth-grade dual language teacher in a Collaborative Team Teaching classroom in New York, NY

Program Description

I work in a dual language Collaborative Team Teaching (CTT) program, where two teachers (one certified in special education and the other in bilingual education) work together within one classroom that combines mainstream students with those who have individualized educational plans (IEPs). It is a unique setting for both teachers and students. Teachers must consider and plan for the demands that learning a second language places on all students simultaneously and for the learning supports that students with learning or language dis/abilities need to be successful in the classroom. For their part, students have a unique opportunity to work with diverse classmates. In our classroom, the interactions between students and the cooperative learning that goes on are not only valuable but also necessary to support the language development of students. In fact, the learning of language takes place throughout the day as students interact with one another and work together.

Facing and Overcoming Challenges

The biggest challenge that I face is making sure that the language and the content of lessons is comprehensible and accessible to *all* students. It is hard to make sure that all students are engaged, that their learning needs are being met, and that they are challenged. To overcome these challenges, I use the Sheltered Instruction Observation Protocol (SIOP) model to plan my lessons. I make sure to incorporate links to prior knowledge, preview unfamiliar vocabulary, and provide visuals. In addition, I feel it is important to differentiate instruction to meet the various learning needs and learning styles of all of our students. When differentiating, as Tomlinson (2002) describes, I decide whether to modify the content (the material the students are learning), the process (the learning experiences that students will participate in), or the product (how the students show their understanding).

Recommendations for Teachers

I have two important suggestions for instructing language learners with dis/abilities. First, never underestimate the importance of visuals or artifacts. For students who are learning a second language, it is helpful to have a picture or an actual object that represents a concept or a new vocabulary word. Incorporating visuals into all lessons will ensure that students do not get stuck on a vocabulary word, but are able to focus on the content of the lesson. In addition, it is important for students to be able to reference this vocabulary; there should be word walls or process charts that incorporate these pictures. This allows students to be surrounded by the language they are in the process of learning, and it will facilitate their language acquisition.

Second, when students are learning a second language, it is important to scaffold language learning by explicitly modeling appropriate language and by providing sentence starters for students. For instance, if students are going to be describing the similarities and differences between two particular objects, then the teacher could model by saying "A similarity between the objects is ____." Then the students should be given a visual reference for the language structure as well as time to practice it. By providing these scaffolds, students will be able to integrate language learning with the content they are learning.

Adaptations for Teaching Bilingual Students With Exceptionalities

- When students are being assessed for learning challenges, pay careful attention to the language(s) of the assessments. A mismatch between the languages of assessment and the students' dominant languages for listening, speaking, reading, and writing can lead to inaccurate results.
- Keep in mind that learning dis/abilities should not be viewed as a barrier to becoming bilingual and biliterate. Students will need additional supports, but learning across two languages should be a viable choice for them, just as it should be for all students.
- Remember that the language the students are learning is being reinforced through interactions with their peers, and encourage interactions between students with exceptionalities and students without exceptionalities.

HERITAGE LANGUAGE PROGRAMS

Marilyn Balluta, Dena'ina Athabascan heritage language teacher in Anchorage, AK

Program Description

I live in Anchorage, Alaska, which is an urban setting. In the public school where I work, four Alaska Native Indigenous language classes are offered to Native students, one of which is Dena'ina Athabascan. The opportunity to teach Dena'ina Athabascan is offered through an evening program specifically designed for Native families. The other opportunity is through a summer enrichment program for kindergarten through eighth grades. Dena'ina Athabascan is indigenous to the Anchorage area.

Facing and Overcoming Challenges

Having enough interest to teach indigenous languages in an urban district is a challenge, as is developing your own curriculum and coming up with new ideas and new methods to teach the native language. I think one of the many challenges Native instructors have in teaching their indigenous language is that they lack the state certification to teach in a classroom, and so they do not receive equitable pay. Most are elderly people who are knowledgeable in their culture and language.

Recommendations for Teachers

I strongly recommend training in culturally appropriate and relevant curriculum. For more focused background on the students and their language and culture, it is also helpful to take summer classes through the American Indian Language Development Institute (AILDI) at the University of Arizona. Last, it is also important to visit your students' villages or reservations, or take a tour. If you are in an urban setting, tour the students' neighborhood.

Adaptations for Teaching in a Heritage Language Program

- Since the range of linguistic abilities in students in heritage language programs varies widely, starting from students' native culture is an important way to begin instruction. As you validate their background, the connections between language and culture will also form.
- Often, students are ashamed of their heritage language and culture, to the extent that they refuse to speak the language or learn about their family's history. Design a heritage project where students interview family members (preferably in the LOTE), gather photographs, and share their stories. This will allow them to see the diversity within their group as they use the language in meaningful ways.
- Shelter and scaffold language in the L2, which, depending on the student population, may be English or the LOTE.
- Integrate language, content, and process in your instruction.

BEFORE-SCHOOL, AFTER-SCHOOL, OR WEEKEND FOREIGN LANGUAGE PROGRAMS

Tulay Tashken, Turkish teacher and principal
for Ataturk School in New York, NY

Program Description

Our weekend program has teachers who are all qualified and have prior experience working with children back in Turkey. This is a great advantage in teaching students about our Turkish heritage and culture. Our teachers have been working at our school for many years and have been consistent with the grades they teach, which is a key factor in maintaining stability and developing their own skills as a teacher. What is also incredibly special is that the students I taught back in 1983 are now bringing their own children to our school, which shows that they are passing the values of the Turkish language, culture, and morals that they learned on to their own children. Our Parent Teacher Association is also very involved with our school and the children overall, which creates an everlasting bond.

Facing and Overcoming Challenges

The biggest challenge that we face is that students do not want to give up their Saturdays because they would rather be home or outside playing with their friends. Many of the students are interested in sports; a majority of them are on their schools' teams, so they give up Saturday practice to come to school. Since class is on a Saturday, students might stay up late on Friday and then come into school very tired and not always wanting to learn, although they catch up quickly. Another problem that the school is currently facing is that we do not really have a classroom environment because we are only on one floor of a building and our classes are partitioned with portable dividers.

In spite of these challenges, students enjoy coming to school because they feel as though it is their second home; they are comfortable with their peers because they are on the same level. In fact, most students tell me they cannot wait for it to be Saturday because it is the day that they get to interact with their peers, and they don't feel intimidated because they might not know the language that well.

Recommendations for Teachers

New teachers must be patient, dedicated, and persistent because they will be sacrificing their own time in order to teach others. Some students require a lot more attention than others, so teachers should be very understanding of different situations because students come from various environments. Children's psychology is another key area that teachers must have a background in because working with children can sometimes be very hard. Teachers who are interested in teaching their own heritage to children should have taught back in their heritage country for a while as well.

Adaptations for Teaching in a Before-School, After-School, or Weekend Foreign Language Program

- Take advantage of the freedom of the program type (especially after-school and on the weekend) to take students to see performances, exhibits, and even foreign films that include the target language and culture. It is also a wonderful opportunity to provide enrichment opportunities that further build on what students are learning in the classroom.

- Teach language through the use of authentic communicative activities, augmented by explicit language instruction.
- Integrate language and content in your instruction whenever possible. Use the arts as a content area. You will be able to shelter and scaffold language as you engage your students in arts-based activities.

SECONDARY FOREIGN LANGUAGE PROGRAMS

Melissa Marinari, high school Spanish teacher for River Dell Regional High School in River Edge, NJ

Program Description

I teach Spanish as a "foreign" language in a suburban public school (Grades 7–12) district about five miles outside of New York City. I say "foreign" because if you are familiar with New York City and its surrounding areas, you know that Spanish (as is the case with many, many other languages) is an intrinsic part of local communities and is not foreign at all. Yet for the majority of my students, speaking anything other than English is, to them, foreign.

In many ways, I think our language program is typical of those across the United States that attempt to instill the value of bilingualism in predominately English-speaking monolinguals. We offer a course of study that focuses on the immediate and practical use of the target language but that also incorporates attention to discrete linguistic structures and the cultural products and practices of those who are native speakers of the target language. However, there are several components of our language program that make what we offer unique. The first is that we give students the opportunity to have six sequential years of language study before graduation. Our middle school program is comprehensive, open to all students, and offered as a full-year course. The students are energetic, physical, and eager learners—the perfect audience for beginning language instruction! The ability to work with this age group every day allows us to create a solid foundation upon which our high school program rests.

The second component that sets us apart from many other programs is that every student in our high school is given a laptop to use for four years. Although this is a recent development in our district, it is already changing the way we teach. The available technology has created many opportunities to connect and communicate in the target language. It has allowed us to assess our students in new and more creative ways, and it has increased our ability to provide differentiated instruction to students that have naturally different language-learning thresholds. I am so appreciative of this opportunity and recognize how privileged we are as a district. Using technology is certainly not the only way to effectively teach language and is not necessarily the best way. As another tool in a teacher's tool kit, however, it can increase student motivation and provide richer, more authentic linguistic practice.

Facing and Overcoming Challenges

The greatest obstacles that I face are societal language ideologies that tend to frame bilingualism as a source of potential problems and that promote English as the only acceptable mode of (public) communication. Since I primarily work with English-speaking monolinguals, I constantly have to contend with the myth that "everyone" already knows or should know English. It is extremely difficult to make the case for bilingualism in a world where English is such a powerful language and where my students have never genuinely had a need to communicate in anything other than English. Moreover, despite a two-year graduation requirement, foreign languages are still considered to be electives in my district (and elsewhere); thus they are not part of the core curriculum like math, science, and English. Labeling foreign language as an elective relegates it to second place and gives the (not so subtle) message to our students that learning another language really isn't a necessary part of becoming an educated citizen—despite frequent claims that our discipline as a whole promotes global citizenship and cross-cultural communication.

To combat these challenges, I work hard to show students that language and language learning are social practices that are infused with cultural and personal meaning related to issues of power, identity, and representation. I feel that learning another language should present students with new ways of seeing themselves and the world. Therefore, my teaching is also influenced by elements of critical language and critical cultural awareness. In my classes, learning Spanish is a gateway into learning about *communication* and about the role that language plays in society. It is also an opportunity to interrogate the relationship between language and culture and to teach students to critically interact with diversity as a way to promote additive bilingualism.

Recommendations for Teachers

I have been teaching Spanish as a foreign language for 14 years and have benefited enormously from the wisdom and advice of several invaluable mentors. My first suggestion to any new language teacher is to seek out, find, or develop meaningful professional relationships with other members of your profession. You will know these people when you meet them. They are the teachers who *love* what they do, who believe in the beauty and complicated nature of language, who truly respect and value their students, and who continue to learn and grow as they teach. The best teachers surround themselves with even better teachers.

My second suggestion is to never lose sight of the big picture. When teaching a (foreign) language, it is very easy to give students the impression that your class is *only* about learning the target language. Your class is about teaching the target language, but it should also be about teaching *about* language and the wonderfully complicated role that it plays in our lives. If you try to explain to your students that knowing Spanish (French, Mandarin, German, etc.) is important, you won't reach anyone other than the students who already think this is the case. To reach the kids who don't immediately buy in, you need to have them experience how language affects them personally in so many ways.

Finally, I would suggest that you never be afraid to show your students how much you love what you do. Have a great time in the classroom, be open to experimentation and failure, and listen to your students. If you do these simple things, you will be modeling every day what it takes to be a good language learner.

Adaptations for Teaching Secondary Foreign Language Instruction

- If students are learning a language of which there are native speakers in the school, pair students up so they can support one another in learning the foreign language and English.
- When native speakers are not available, use the Internet to locate a Web site that will partner students from your classroom with students from other countries in order to be pen pals or e-mail pals. This will allow students to have real-world literacy experiences.
- Foreign language education has been dominated by explicit language instruction. While this is an important part of learning an additional language, it's also critical for students to develop oral proficiency—ideally through authentic situations. Be careful not to fall into the trap of drill-and-kill; also build in time for students to use the language among themselves and with others.

- Use newspapers to expose students to current events at the local and international level. Print media are often written at a reading level that is accessible to advanced to intermediate students.
- Teach language through the use of authentic communicative activities, augmented by explicit language instruction.
- Integrate language and content in your instruction whenever possible. Use the arts as a content area. You will be able to shelter and scaffold language as you engage your students in arts-based activities.

PRIVATE SCHOOL PROGRAMS

In this section, we discuss three variations of private school programs that include second language instruction as part of the curriculum. We include separate contributions from educators from differing programs, but make recommendations for adaptations to private school practice collectively at the end of this section.

SECULAR SECOND LANGUAGE PROGRAMS IN PRIVATE SCHOOLS

Elisabeth Heurtefeu, former teacher and elementary school director for Lycée Français de Chicago in Chicago, IL; current principal of LaSalle Language Academy in Chicago, IL

Program Description

The uniqueness of our program resides in enrolling students as early as three years old and in following the French national curriculum, in French, with students who are English speakers. In France, public schools start at the preschool level, as soon as the children are toilet trained. Actually, more and more students are enrolled at two and a half years old and spend four years in preschool (until the end of kindergarten) before moving on to another location for elementary (first through fifth grades).

At the Lycée Français in Chicago, students work with teachers who are certified in France. Most are born in France and follow a full-immersion program. Seventy percent of the students enrolled at the preschool level are born in the United States and speak English at home. Only in kindergarten, after two years of full immersion, do they start one period of English per day. Students learn phonics in both languages and learn to read both languages in kindergarten and first grade. Most students are fluent in French by the end of fourth grade and speak like native French individuals.

Facing and Overcoming Challenges

In preschool, the challenge is to make sure students who have just mastered their first language do not get frustrated when learning a new language. Research shows that it is important to offer support in the mother language because the child will tend to be more proficient in the second language if he or she already has a rich vocabulary in the first language. The other challenge is to plan learning situations so that students can make sense of what is going on and learn the language painlessly. In the first two years, some students may listen more than they speak.

Recommendations for Teachers

Involve parents in reinforcing the language spoken at home; ask them to read a lot to their child to improve vocabulary in the mother tongue. At school, try to mime some words instead of translating, speak the language as much as possible without translating, and use a lot of songs, rhymes, and acting out of favorite books that students are familiar with in both languages. When acting out stories, students master essential sentence structures and vocabulary painlessly. If a child does not understand the new language, request that another child translate so that the teacher is perceived as only speaking the target language.

SECULAR SECOND LANGUAGE PROGRAMS IN RELIGIOUS SCHOOLS

Brigid Burke, PhD, former Catholic school French teacher for Mount Carmel High School in Chicago, IL; current assistant professor of foreign language education at Bowling Green State University in Bowling Green, OH

Program Description

My French program was unique in that I did not have to work with other French teachers at my school. There were three Spanish teachers and one Latin teacher, but I was the only French teacher. This position allowed me to clarify my short-term and long-term goals and teach students with those in mind.

In many cases, teachers in public schools experience resistance from students and colleagues when they try to implement communicative language teaching, which in its purest form involves teaching the world language through immersion. They usually give in to the resistance and do not end up using the methods they want to use when teaching world language. Even though I experienced a bit of resistance from some more advanced French students at the beginning, the administration supported my teaching approach, and I was able to help students develop their communicative competence in French. The administrators at the Catholic school in which I taught supported their teachers and did not impose their agendas on our teaching. I wanted other teachers to be informed of the methods I used with secondary students so that they could use them themselves. The administration allowed me the freedom to implement curriculum and instruction even if it was different from the norm. By inviting the principal and assistant principal into my classroom from time to time, I was able to show them that students were able to speak and write in French, even at the novice level.

Facing and Overcoming Challenges

The only challenge I faced was in my first year of teaching: resistance from the advanced-level French students to being asked to always speak French. One French 4 student dropped my class because I asked him to use his French on a daily basis. The instructor who had taught for three years before me had used the grammar-translation method. I used the communicative approach and expected students to *use* French inside and outside of my classroom. I overcame this resistance by sticking to my plan of using immersion and promoting communicative language teaching. Each year, I was able to help students learn French. Students were amazed at their ability to use their French in a short amount of time. At the end of French 1, they were able to have short conversations and write paragraphs about various topics. Eventually, parents wanted to enroll their children in my classes because they had heard that the children would actually learn French. My program grew in numbers after being at the school for two years.

To develop my language skills and keep current with Francophone culture, I was able to visit France each summer. I lived with my French family, whom I had met on my first visit to France. On each visit, I made a point of visiting a new region in France so I could bring new knowledge back to my students. One summer, I met a woman from Quebec, whom I then visited the following spring break.

Recommendations for Teachers

If you are in a school where you are the only teacher for a particular language, you need to be ready for some resistance to your methods. For the first two years, you will be working very hard on your many preps and on selling your program to the students and their parents. Be sure that you feel comfortable with the administration when you sign your contract, and keep them informed of your successes and your difficulties. Invite the principal in to see your students in action, using the world language. By doing this, the administration will be able to speak knowledgeably about your program with parents, thus showing support. Finally, if you are teaching in a Catholic school, do not be afraid to ask for more money. I was able to fill my classroom with wonderful materials each year for students to improve their language.

RELIGIOUS SECOND LANGUAGE PROGRAMS

Ariel Stone, rabbi of Congregation Shir Tikvah and Hebrew religious school teacher for over 25 years in Miami, FL; New York, NY; Kiev, Ukraine; Atlanta, GA; and currently in Portland, OR

Program Description

Hebrew taught in a religious context is not so much a language for conversation as it is a powerful religious symbol. The primary goal of a religious Hebrew school is to help a student become fluent in basic Jewish religious literacy goals: to be able to navigate the Jewish prayer book and to be able to read from the Torah. This is not the same as learning a language for conversation. Hebrew learned for ritual purposes may not be taught for comprehension but rather for what is called decoding, the ability to accurately vocalize the letters and vowels of the Hebrew alphabet.

Facing and Overcoming Challenges

Teaching a language in a religious context is an activity shadowed by the larger relationship the student has with the religion itself. Beyond this psychological challenge, teaching Hebrew decoding requires a special focus upon the skill of memorizing the letters and their sounds rather than developing the vocabulary of a spoken language. Memory games and other forms of reinforcement of decoding skills help a great deal. (Think of it as similar to teaching Morse code.) Some religious school Hebrew programs include basic conversational Hebrew in order to make the content more relevant, and therefore more interesting, to the average student; there are some basic language phrases that do coincide with liturgical Hebrew.

Recommendations for Teachers

Teachers should use as many of the different intelligences as possible to keep what is very simple material from becoming boring. They should also incorporate conversational phrases whenever possible. Last, it is important not to ignore the larger religious context—use it in whatever positive and reinforcing ways are possible.

Adaptations for Teaching in Private Schools (Secular and Religious)

- Teach language through the use of authentic communicative activities, augmented by explicit language instruction.
- Integrate language and content in your instruction whenever possible. If your school uses a curricular model in which language is taught separately from content, consider using the arts as a content area. You will be able to shelter and scaffold language as you engage your students in arts-based activities.
- If you teach in a private immersion school, shelter and scaffold language in the L2 and integrate language, content, and process in your instruction.
- If the target language is intertwined with a religious context, make certain that linguistic and religious connections are not ignored but, rather, incorporated with instruction to enrich teaching and learning.

CONCLUDING THOUGHTS

Bilingual education is a broad field with a range of programs that educate students in the areas of language, culture, and academic content, and in addition, may impact self-esteem, identity construction, and quality of life. As in any other field, there is no one magical approach to teaching and learning. For a teacher in any given program, it is critical to consider the needs of your students and the goals of the program as you put curricular and pedagogical accommodations in place. Doing so will ensure that your students receive a linguistically and culturally relevant education.

REFERENCES

Hélot, C., & Young, A. (2006). Imagining multilingual education in France: A language and awareness project at the primary level. In O. García, T. Skutnabb-Kangas, & M. E. Torres-Guzmán (Eds.), *Imagining multilingual schools: Languages in education and globalization* (pp. 69–90). Clevedon, England: Multilingual Matters.

Tomlinson, C. A. (2002). Different learners, different lessons. *Scholastic Instructor.* 112(2), 21–26.

9

Equity and Advocacy

Essential Question

How does being a bilingual teacher make me different?

> ### One Teacher's Dilemma
>
> When I started, it really angered me when the principal said, "There's no glory in bilingual education." I remember this so well because I was so angry when he said it. And we never got any extra equipment, like all these art-in-the-studio programs. The bilingual students didn't get to participate in all these things until about four or five years ago.

Tung, who teaches Chinese students, recounts his early experiences as a teacher. He quickly discovered that not only bilingual teachers but also bilingual students were relegated to second-class status. Even more problematic was how some of the students internalized their own marginalization.

One kid, himself, said, "As bilingual students we are not the regular students, we are bilingual students." But the kids, the regular kids say, "Oh, these are the bilingual kids, the stupid bilingual kids." These things still happen.

Tung highlights the negative perceptions that are held toward bilingual education and the paltry resources often given to the field. This is ironic because becoming a bilingual teacher requires additional professional preparation, not just in terms of language skills but also in terms of curriculum and pedagogy. In addition, bilingual teachers must be able to teach in multiple contexts, from mainstream to multilingual classrooms. Yet they are often marginalized within their schools, just as bilingual education is often stigmatized in the public eye. Contrary to such misperceptions, bilingual education is a multifaceted, multidisciplinary field, and bilingual teachers play a pivotal role in promoting educational equity in the United States. Rather than being marginalized, they should be valued. This chapter highlights how being a bilingual teacher not only makes educators different, but also makes them important in ways that go beyond the world of the classroom.

THE POLITICS OF BILINGUAL EDUCATION

The debate over bilingual education in the United States is framed in terms of curriculum, effectiveness, and other traditional educational criteria. Answers to many of the objections about bilingual education are available, and research largely supports the contentions of the advocates of bilingual education. Objective data on bilingual programs are ineffective in resolving the underlying issue of the debate, however. Most of the emotional heat over bilingual education is generated by the official recognition of ethnicity as a special status in public education. The conflict can be resolved either by convincing the public of the pedagogical value of bilingual education or by diluting its association with ethnicity and making functional bilingualism the goal for all students. (Hakuta, 1986, p. 233)

Kenji Hakuta's discussion of the underlying politics of bilingual education, written in 1986, still holds true today. We agree with his premise that the American public does not necessarily look at language as the key issue in bilingual education but rather at ethnicity. We would add that public emotions regarding ethnicity push buttons similar to the lightning rod of race. Crawford and Krashen (2007) remind us that "bilingual education raises a host of larger questions, such as immigrant rights and responsibilities, the role of English in our society, and even what it means to be an American" (p. 59). Hakuta (1986) asserts that this heated debate will not be resolved until we either manage to pull the ethnicity card out of bilingual education, or make bilingualism a valuable prize to be sought after by all students.

The factors of race and class, in addition to ethnicity, further complicate the politically vulnerable status of bilingual education. Most children served by bilingual educational programs are students of color from low-income backgrounds. By contrast, bilingual schools outside the United States are typically viewed as institutions for serving the privileged students whose parents view bilingualism as a career asset.

As bilingual educators, we should not only be cognizant of the gifts that bilingualism brings; we should also be staunch advocates for educational equity. It is important to understand that, in addition to enhanced opportunities for communication and advantages in the job market, bilingualism can bring cognitive and academic benefits, stronger connections to family and community, and positive identity construction (Reyes & Vallone, 2007). In addition, because we work with marginalized students and communities, we must be attuned to issues of social justice. The field of multicultural education was born out of the civil rights movement of the 1960s, and the Bilingual Education Act of 1968 was passed during that era. So it is not surprising that bilingual educators have been deeply involved in struggles for educational equity.

Naturally, being part of a field that is so politically charged makes us different. We cannot think of our work as merely a job, because that work has a broader social significance. And we must share that understanding with our students and their families, yet we cannot take for granted that they will automatically and enthusiastically embrace bilingual education. We must think carefully about how we collaborate with families, especially in light of the continuing controversy surrounding bilingual education.

TRY THIS!

Elementary and Secondary Levels

All parents want the best education for their children. Selecting bilingual or ESL programs is an important decision that parents make in many states. Unfortunately, the information they receive about such programs may not always be based on research and sound pedagogy. To help families make informed decisions, bilingual educators should play a role explaining these programs. Suggest that the school or district hold bilingual events in which families can learn about the goals and differences of bilingual and ESL programs. Discuss the following topics:

- Different models of bilingual education (e.g., one- or two-way bilingual immersion, transitional, heritage language) and ESL (e.g., pull out, push-in/collaborative team teaching) and the language and content goals of each
- Benefits of bilingualism (e.g., cross-cultural, cognitive, economic, global)
- Research on the time necessary to learn a language for academic purposes

- Research on academic outcomes of students who are in well-implemented bilingual and ESL programs
- How these different programs actually function—invite families into classrooms to see them

Orchestrating this type of event for families is a lot of work and should be done in collaboration with teachers, administrators, and district personnel. Students who are part of these programs can also talk about their experiences, as can their families.

COLLABORATING WITH FAMILIES FOR THE BENEFIT OF CHILDREN

Bilingual teachers often encounter a close, familial-like bond with students and their families, with whom they share a common language and, often, a common culture. When students must negotiate a new language and culture, it comes as a huge relief to learn that their teacher understands their background. Families may experience similar feelings, opening the door for interactions and collaboration.

We know from a variety of studies that parental involvement results in positive academic outcomes for students (Jeynes, 2005). But looking only at parents is limiting especially when students have nontraditional family arrangements and transnational lives; such an approach favors the dominant American perspective of care-giving as solely a function of the nuclear family. Many other cultures, however, value the direct involvement of extended family members such as grandparents, aunts, uncles, older siblings, and even family friends as a crucial part of the child-rearing experience. Another point of cultural divergence is the meaning of education across different groups. For many Latinos, education goes beyond academics and good grades and includes things like behavior, morals, respect, and interpersonal relationships (Delgado-Gaitan, 2004). The way families involve themselves in the educational process is yet another area where cultural differences come into play as Maurice, a Haitian Creole bilingual teacher, explains:

> In Haiti, parents don't get involved. In school, we [the teachers] do everything, we discipline, we don't need the parents. There is something in Haiti called a *carte blanche*, it's like a white slip to do whatever you want. But they think the same thing here; the school can do all these things. They don't really get involved. And not only that, it's because of the language, too.

Such families see a clear divide between the home and the school, whereas in U.S. schools the ideal is one of partnership and collaboration. The parents of bilingual students may focus primarily on ensuring that their child is taken care of and well-behaved in school. When families do not play an active role in their child's schooling it is often (mis)attributed to long work hours or multiple jobs, concerns about not being able to communicate in English, or even a fear of being "found out" for undocumented families. Yet they may actually feel they are acting appropriately, reflecting culturally divergent assumptions from those of educators.

While the commonalities across languages and cultures will certainly be a critical factor in communicating and collaborating with families, there is still a need to bridge the home-school environments. The first step is to invite families to teach us about our students and their backgrounds, a subject about which they are clearly the best source of information. In the beginning of the year, Christina, a first-grade Spanish dual language teacher, schedules interviews with her students' parents to learn about their children. (For those who cannot come in, she sends home questionnaires). She positions the parents as experts and values their knowledge. Throughout the year, she also works with them on understanding how the school and classroom function, especially when it differs from their country of origin. Thus, both the teachers and families can learn from and teach one another, with the student at the heart of the two-way collaboration.

TRY THIS!

Elementary and Secondary Level

Invite families for a "teach the teacher" event. Create a questionnaire (either in the L1 or bilingually) that asks families to share information about their child. Questions to ask can include:

- Who are the primary caregivers? What is their relationship to the child?
- Which languages are spoken at home? Who speaks the languages? What is the student's language preference?
- What are the student's activities and responsibilities outside of school?
- What are the student's likes and dislikes?
- What is the best way to motivate your child?
- Do you have any behavioral, academic, or health concerns regarding your child?
- What do you want for your child this year?

In addition to these specific questions, have families think about information they would feel comfortable sharing with the class, such as general skills, international experiences, cultural traditions, and songs. Remind them that they can speak in any language in which they feel comfortable.

Beyond helping teachers learn about their children, families bring a wealth of knowledge that can be shared and used in the classroom for teaching and learning. While some families have a significant amount of formal education, which is typically valued in schools, others bring with them numerous skills that can also be transferred into academics. Teacher-researchers have uncovered expertise in areas that span from agriculture to business to household management to medicine. These are referred to as *funds of knowledge,* or the resources and knowledge found in households that are often viewed as poverty stricken and lacking in academic skills (González, Moll, & Amanti, 2005). When we consider carefully what families bring, by conducting home visits or even just by asking questions, we find that parents can contribute to a wide range of content areas by sharing their real-world experiences. We can involve our families in a science unit on farming, a math unit on measuring, or a social studies unit on world religions, to name just a few examples. Beyond asking parents to come into school (which is not always possible with job and family responsibilities), we can include these funds of knowledge as a key part of the curriculum and even as a way to connect content and standards with our students' realities. In the following passage, Dolores explains how she brings in the experiences of her students and their families to create a collaborative unit on immigration in New York City:

> What I do is that everything we do in immigration, we relate it to the children's experiences. During that unit they not only study what happened on Ellis Island, but how their family got here, why their family came. What did their family have to do to get to this country, what language was the school in, what was their experience at school, etc. They look at all the things from the country they came from. This year as our class project we did an immigration quilt, which was called "Treasures from Home," and each family contributed. I made it a family project so families came to the classroom and they worked together on making a panel for the quilt. And it was choosing something important from their family, from their culture that they brought to this country or another family brought to this country. Then parents had to write a piece about their experiences and kids had to write a piece explaining the panel and why they chose that panel.

STRESSING THE IMPORTANCE OF THE NATIVE LANGUAGE

Bilingual programs work against the tide of English-only assimilation to foster bilingualism and multiculturalism in our students. While the role of schools is critical to this charge, we cannot succeed without the support of families and communities (Fishman, 1991). Just the fact that the families of your students have opted to place them in a bilingual program is a great start. However, there is a lot of negative (mis)information regarding native language use and bilingualism circulating in the media. Too often, families of emergent bilingual students are told to speak more English at home as a means of increasing their proficiency. The following anecdote, recounted by a former Spanish bilingual teacher, illustrates the danger implicit in parents speaking to children in only their nondominant language:

> I met Javier when was I was in charge of administering the Language Assessment Scales (LAS) for my school district. Javier was in fourth grade at the time. I gave him the LAS first in English, and he scored nondominant. I wasn't surprised. That was typically how Mexican students who were sent to me for testing scored. Then, I tested him in Spanish. What a shock . . . he came out non-dominant in Spanish, too! I was much younger then, and less experienced, so I had never seen anything like that before. I couldn't figure it out. Finally I decided to see if his parents would come in and talk to me about it, and they did. It was difficult for them to speak English so we spoke in Spanish. I asked them what language they spoke with Javier at home, and to my surprise, they said English! When I asked them why they didn't speak to him in Spanish, they said they came here to give a better life to their son, and that they decided to speak in English to him all the time, to help him have a better life here.

Contrary to the decision of the parents in the above vignette, prominent researcher Catherine Snow (1997) maintains parents can best support their child(ren)'s education by speaking to them in their native tongue. One of the most important gifts that families can give their children is the gift of language. The specific language is immaterial; rather, it is fluency in language that is important. Fluent language allows students to communicate in complex and sophisticated ways that will jump-start their learning additional languages, such as English. As a way to encourage families to continue the development and use of their native language, The Twenty-First Century Academy (a dual language public school in New York City) holds book clubs for parents where adult literature is selected in Spanish to read and discuss collectively. These clubs are similar to what older students experience in their language arts classes. As a result of participating in them, family members attain firsthand knowledge regarding their children's learning processes, which often differ from the traditional approaches used in their countries of origin. In this manner, families can better support their children's educational experience and also maintain their native language literacy.

The earlier families can get information about the cultural, cognitive, social, and economic benefits of bilingualism and bilingual education, the better. An innovative program in Wales provides parents of infants with pamphlets that outline a range of reasons to speak to their child in the native language (Welsh), as well as the numerous advantages of being bilingual (Edwards & Newcombe, 2006). Since bilingual educators tend to have strong bonds with families, you may be in a position to confer with parents about not only your students, but about the native language use, development, and eventual bilingualism of their younger siblings. This information is especially critical because they constantly receive contradictory "English only" messages from news media and many state and national policy makers. Districts and schools can create informative brochures that dispel myths about bilingual education, and hold sessions that outline the process of (second) language teaching and learning. Many immigrant parents are especially concerned about their children learning English, or not learning English quickly enough. We can share findings about the importance of a foundation in the L1 and its positive impact on second language development (Cummins, 1991). Families may also need reassurance that bilingual programs are equally concerned with students' learning English.

Even when schools and families stress the importance of the native language, students often get the message early on that English is the language of power. Students may develop a strong preference for English, resist speaking their L1, and grimace when it's time for instruction in that language. Thus, it is important for students to understand the importance of being bilingual and biliterate. At the start of the school year, we can talk with students about why they are in a bilingual classroom and how that offers unique opportunities. Rosario, a fifth-grade dual language teacher, tells her students,

> to be proud of who they are, never to forget where they come from, where their parents come from. And their language, never to be ashamed of who they are and their language because they are very important . . . they are not less than anybody else. On the contrary, they have more to offer.

In Figure 9.1, Matthew Moon, a first-grade Korean-English bilingual student, shows through his artwork and related comments the importance of speaking more than one language. Matthew (the little boy on the right) says to the robot in Korean, "Hi, what are you?" and the robot responds, "Um, what did you say?" When he explained this picture to his mother, he told her that the robot didn't even understand the simple word *hi*. That's because the robot didn't take the time to learn Korean. Even at an early age, Mathew realizes the importance of learning your native language! Through activities as simple as drawing a picture, students can be encouraged to think through the ways in which speaking multiple languages can be meaningful in their lives.

Figure 9.1

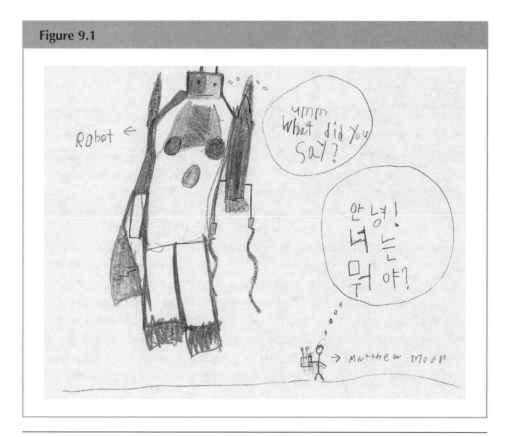

Source: Created by Matthew Moon. Used with permission.

TRY THIS!

Elementary and Secondary Level

Make sure important and special events in and out of the school are also held in the L1. For example, bring in guest speakers, hold science fairs and plays or assemblies in the LOTE. When going on field trips, try to include shows, exhibitions, and guides that can communicate with students in their L1. This will allow students to experience the value of their native language in their school and in their community.

TRY THIS!

Elementary

Have students interview bilingual individuals in the school and in the community. Ask them questions related to how being bilingual is helpful for them. Categorize the reasons, and then have students create bilingual brochures that list and describe the various advantages of being bilingual. These can be circulated throughout the school, to families, and even throughout the community. This project will allow students to become researchers and advocates for multilingualism.

TRY THIS!

Secondary

Have students investigate job ads. Analyze the types of jobs that require bilingualism and cross-cultural knowledge, as well as why these linguistic and cultural skills are in demand. Discuss the connection to bilingual programs and future success.

Bilingual education and even bilingualism have been under fire in the United States for many decades. Families can be powerful advocates for bilingual teachers and programs because they can often voice issues that would be difficult for teachers to speak about without reprimand or risk to their jobs. Even parents who are not accustomed to speaking up may exhibit enormous courage when it comes to doing what is best for their children's education. It was a group of parents who, in 1974, brought the landmark *Lau v. Nichols* case to the Supreme Court, which ruled in their favor and required schools to provide language minority students with appropriate learning environments. The role of families cannot be underestimated as we fight to keep and expand spaces for bilingual programs.

NEGOTIATING PRESSURE TO TEACH TO THE TEST

High-stakes standardized testing is now prevalent across our nation, and it is having major effects on classroom instruction—in particular, *teaching to the test*. Menken (2008, p. 118) describes this phenomenon as "focusing instruction on test content and skills or, more explicitly . . . devoting class time to teaching test items and test taking strategies." Teaching to the test has become increasingly common as the stakes associated with standardized tests, such as grade promotion and graduation, have increased over time—especially under No Child Left Behind (NCLB). Because standardized testing in all likelihood will be a part of U.S.

educational culture for many years to come, simply resisting the pressure to teach to the test is not enough. Allowing students to critically explore the rationale behind standardized tests, including the ways in which they have been used to create racial, ethnic, and socioeconomic stratification, can promote deep thinking and provide motivation for students to do well on such tests.

Although standardized tests are neither fair nor necessarily related to developing life-long learning skills, scoring well on them is a requirement for success in today's schools. Once students understand their underlying inequities, an opening for test preparation is created. In the following vignette, a third-grade teacher explains the reality of high-stakes tests to her students:

> My students enjoy coming to school. We have a classroom community here. Virtually everything we do is based on some type of authentic learning situation. So when I have to get them ready for standardized tests, I have a real problem. I cannot justify this activity within the framework I have set up in my classroom. So I made up a game. I told my kids that there is a group of old men sitting around in a private room, trying to think up ways of tricking kids into doing poorly on tests. I even did some funny little dramatizations of how they talk to each other. But then I told my kids that I knew some tricks we could use, to trick them instead of them tricking us. That's how I got them into learning how to take these tests. It became a game. I said we could make those old men really angry if we did really well on the tests because it would mean that we out-smarted them!

While we cannot avoid preparing our students for standardized tests, we do have choice in how to do so. In determining the best approach for your students, consider their ages and other contextual factors. Then, use your creativity and intellect to devise an approach best suited to your own unique classroom.

TRY THIS!

Secondary Level

Often, due to schools with poorly staffed counseling departments, high school students do not get the necessary information related to the college admissions process. To prepare students for this difficult stage and to allow them to understand the role of standardized testing in college admissions, ask students to research the tests that different colleges require for admission. Also, ask students to look into which schools have dropped standardized tests such as the SAT in favor of more holistic admission requirements. Have the class debate the reasons for and against using such tests as a central aspect of admissions decisions.

Approaches to teaching to the test vary. Some schools integrate testing strategies into regular classroom instruction. Others take an approach that consists of teaching required skills and strategies directly or through a prepackaged and scripted test-prep program with simulated test questions. Many schools, especially those with minority students and those in low-income areas, invest a great deal of money and time into one or both of these direct approaches. While teaching to the test may help students increase their scores, they simultaneously lose out on learning about content that is not tested and may experience disconnected learning focused on isolated skills and strategies (Kohn, 2002; Meier, 2002; Menken, 2008; Valenzuela, 2005).

It is impossible to do well on a test without acquiring the content that is tested or the strategies required to deduce the correct answer. There are, however, meaningful and relevant ways to prepare students for this experience. When appropriate, teachers can give attention to connections between content and students' experiences and backgrounds. Test-taking strategies can be integrated into content learning. For example, students can read passages and answer questions using a text being read with a unit of study. In addition, instruction involving concepts and strategies can be done in the native language of the students, as these concepts and strategies will transfer to English.

TRY THIS!

Elementary and Secondary Level

Take a unit of study that you have already developed, and place it side-by-side with a list of skills and strategies required for the standardized test(s) your students must take. Look for areas where you can highlight the skills and strategies required for the test. This way, you can continue with the regular course of study, but still include the areas students require to be successful on the tests. Just make sure that, once it comes time to take the tests, students have been exposed to most of the required skills.

While it's impossible to completely avoid teaching to the test given the current high-stakes environment, we must also be cognizant of teaching to the whole child. This means providing students with broad exposure to all areas: the core content, the arts, technology, and enrichment studies. The obstacle to creating a comprehensive program often boils down to a lack of time. Therefore, integration of subject areas becomes key. For instance, there are many opportunities to combine language arts (in English or the LOTE) with social studies. You can read historical fiction books aloud, and students can write journals from the perspective of a person from the time period being studied. Math and science also have natural connections that, if planned carefully, can maximize learning as students are given double the exposure to related content vocabulary and interconnected concepts. Thematic learning, where a topic is covered across all the content areas, is especially beneficial for ELLs because it develops their languages in that area and deepens their understanding of the selected topic (Freeman, Freeman, & Mercuri, 2005). For example, a thematic unit on the ancient Mayans of Mesoamerica could explore their languages and writing systems for language arts, their use of astronomy and creation of calendars for science, an in-depth look at their devised counting system and building structures such as pyramids for math, an exploration into their social organization of communities for social studies, and their style of painting, ceramics, and sculptures for art. In planning for such a thematic unit, attention would be given to meeting local or state standards as well as embedding skills and strategies for testing.

Testing and teaching have become a difficult balancing act that is especially challenging for bilingual teachers. Marleine, a third-grade Haitian Creole bilingual teacher in a transitional program of bilingual instruction, explains how she handles the pressures in spite of top-down demands to teach test skills in the language of the test:

> I have a bilingual class; I have to teach the children language. I am going to teach two and a half days in Creole and two and a half days in English. But they [the district personnel] say the test is in English and I am not preparing the students for the test. I am not teaching to the test, I am teaching children for life. When children can function in their own language, it will be very easy for the child to transition into English. I have to explain this to them.

As a bilingual teacher, you will undoubtedly come across mandates, including but not limited to standardized testing, that can compromise the efficacy of bilingual education and students' learning. We can either let our concerns be pent up in our classrooms and among colleagues who hold similar views, or we can become vocal advocates who stand up for the professionalism of teachers and their right to make pedagogical decisions and educate others about the unique needs of bilingual learners. Similarly, we must allow our students to develop critical perspectives about inequitable systemic structures, helping to prepare them to overcome similar obstacles they may face later in life.

ADVOCATING FOR BILINGUALISM AT THE SCHOOL, DISTRICT, AND COMMUNITY LEVEL

> Probably, I would [question or challenge policies] if I would think it's one of the main matters for me, but I never thought there is something that needed to be changed, so I don't think so. We never really open our mouths, to be frank.

Russian bilingual teacher Beth describes what has become far too commonplace for bilingual educators: lack of participation in the local school decision-making processes. This is often the result of a top-down approach to how and what teachers must teach. The words of Chinese bilingual teacher Xi illustrate what happens when bilingual educators do find their voice. They often learn that if they question school policies, they can expect a lack of concern and institutional inaction.

> They [the administration] tell us what to do. They asked me to do the third-grade curriculum, so I cannot do anything, even though I have third and fourth graders. But sometimes I feel bad for them [the students], so I need to do something to make sure they understand. . . . I mentioned it to my supervisor during the beginning of the year, but she told me she cannot do anything.

The questions here are as follows: How do we find both our individual and collective voices to advocate for bilingual education and hence educational equity in our schools, districts, and communities? And how can we do so without sacrificing our own jobs and careers?

Countless conversations with bilingual educators, combined with a wealth of personal experiences, have convinced us that individual activism is a difficult road to travel. Collective advocacy is not only safer, but also more effective. As noted previously, parents can often be exceedingly powerful allies. Community and professional organizations also play a vital role in advocacy, and maintaining a voice in the media is crucial to changing human perspectives over time. It is at the local school level, however, that much advocacy is born and propelled forward to a larger arena. This is illustrated in the recent research of Karyn Mallet, who describes the process that many educators have gone through as they learn to advocate for their bilingual students. In the proposed Heuristic for Advocacy Among English Language Professionals (ELPs), Mallett (2009) puts forward a structured framework in which research-based knowledge and classroom experience are positively linked to advocacy-oriented efforts (p. 176). (Although the proposed Heuristic for Advocacy is geared for ELPs, we would argue that it is equally viable for bilingual educators who work in and through two or more languages. After all, being an ELP is one of the primary roles of being a bilingual teacher.)

The model, comprised of five interwoven and nonsequential stages, outlines five stages that propel us toward active advocacy and gives examples of what happens at each level. A summary of her findings is listed here:

Stage One—Inquiry: Recognizing a problem that is negatively affecting ELLs and/or ELPs (English language professionals) at the local, state and/or national level

- Taking part in informal conversations about problematic issues related to aspects of professional practices
- Reflecting on institutional, local, state, or national forms of discrimination
- Noticing unfair practices that affect ELLs and/or ELPs
- Being asked to address a language-related social issue that is unfamiliar

Stage Two—Consciousness: Gathering information related to the recognized problem that is negatively affecting ELLs and/or ELPs at the local, state, and/or national level

- Forming common-cause coalitions
- Joining professional groups
- Participating in discussions
- Conducting primary and secondary research to further understanding of the issue
- Asking questions

Stage Three—Critique: Addressing the recognized problem that is negatively affecting ELLs and/or ELPs at the local, state, and /or national level

- Delivering a conference research paper
- Discussing issues with like-minded people
- Supporting and inspiring research and advocacy among other ELPs
- Arguing one's perspective with opposing parties
- Listening to and respecting those who have different views

Stage Four—Vision: Constructing a plan to ameliorate the recognized problem that is negatively affecting ELLs and/or ELPs at the local, state, and/or national level

- Contacting decision maker(s) in order to establish communication
- Bypassing or pushing past gate keepers
- Collaborating with others regarding details of the proposed plan for action/change
- Preparing to meet with decision makers
- Assessing audience in terms of how issues should be framed and what data will be persuasive

Stage Five—Action: Communicating with decision makers a specific plan designed to address the recognized problem that is negatively affecting ELLs and/or ELPs at the local, state, and/or national level

- Informing the public about the problem and what is needed to improve the current situation
- Keeping issue-relevant information in the forefront of others' minds

Mallet (2009) clearly delineates the process that brings so many bilingual educators from reflection to action. Her research readily translates into an action plan for bilingual educators who want to make a real difference in the lives of students and families: Understand what problems ELLs face in the educational system, communicate this information, propose solutions at all levels, and never let up. We would add that advocacy takes just as much energy and creativity as good teaching. Context is every bit as important in advocacy as it is in the classroom. Ultimately, every situation may require a somewhat unique plan. But do not go it alone. Seek out the support of other educators, parents, and community members. Try to get the media in your court. And remember that advocacy and educational equity go hand in hand. That is one of the reasons why bilingual educators are different.

Return to the Essential Question

How does being a bilingual teacher make me different?

Beyond the obvious ways in which bilingual teachers differ from mainstream teachers, such as teaching in and through two languages, there are sociopolitical factors that require bilingual teachers to go beyond teaching and into advocacy. This may require educating and working with families to stand up for programs that allow students to build on their strengths, specifically the linguistic and cultural backgrounds that they bring to school. In the following vignette, a teacher explains how a bilingual program could have easily been transitioned into an English-only program if she and her colleagues had not taken action.

One Teacher's Response

The principal of my school tried to dismantle the native language component of our bilingual program. There were two of us there. My colleague Gloria was from Guatemala and was strongly Spanish dominant. She taught the native language part of the program. I taught the ESL curriculum. So the principal sent Gloria to another school and brought in his friend, who was a teacher but had no background whatsoever in bilingual education or even ESL. I was supposed to teach her how to teach ESL. So I told the principal that I could help her with ESL, but then I would have to teach the Spanish curriculum and I was only conversational in Spanish. So he said, "Then teach ESL." And I reminded him that the kids were supposed to have instruction in their native language, but he didn't care. He said only the English curriculum was important anyway. Well, it was the first year of school reform in Chicago, and the Local School Council (LSC) had a lot of control in school policy; they even controlled the contract of the principal. So I called a meeting of the Bilingual Parents Council by myself. Without Gloria, I was afraid to speak in front of a whole group of adults in Spanish, but I did it anyway, and they appreciated it, and they were angry about what was going on. So we sort of went underground and organized the bilingual parents and community, and we took control of the Local School Council at the next election, and then *we* had the power! It was tricky because I didn't want to lose my job, but since the LSC was the boss of the principal, they protected me. It was one of the most amazing experiences of my life.

Although this event, described by Samantha, an ESL teacher, is unique, it describes what can happen when parents are empowered by educators to advocate for their children. Advocating for our bilingual students and their families not only takes dedication, integrity, and creativity; it also takes strategic thinking and courage. Not all stories end as successfully as the one described above. Yet effective advocacy such as this can give us the hope and inspiration we need to do the important work that we do each day. Sometimes we are lucky enough to see these stories reflected in the written words of our students.

REFERENCES

Crawford, J. W., & Krashen, S. (2007). *English learners in American classrooms: 101 questions 101 answers.* New York: Scholastic.

Cummins, J. (1991). Interdependence of first- and second-language proficiency in bilingual children. In E. Biaystock (Ed.), *Language processing in bilingual children* (pp. 70–89). Cambridge, UK: Cambridge University Press.

Delgado-Gaitan, C. (2004). *Involving Latino families in schools: Raising achievement through home-school partnerships.* Thousand Oaks, CA: Corwin.

Edwards, V., & Newcombe, L. P. (2006). Back to basics: Marketing the benefits of bilingualism. In O. García, T. Skutnabb-Kangas, & M. E. Torres-Guzmán (Eds.), *Imagining multilingual schools: Languages in education and globalization* (pp. 137–149). Clevedon, England: Multilingual Matters.

Fishman, J. (1991). *Reversing language shift: Theoretical and empirical foundations of assistance to threatened languages.* Clevedon: Multilingual Matters.

Freeman, Y. S., Freeman, D. E., & Mercuri, S. P. (2005). *Dual language essentials for teachers and administrators.* Portsmouth, NH: Heinemann.

González, N. E., Moll, L., & Amanti, C. (Eds). (2005). *Funds of knowledge: Theorizing practices in households and classrooms.* Mahwah, NJ: Lawrence Erlbaum.

Hakuta, K. (1986). *Mirror of language: The debate on bilingualism.* Basic Books.

Jeynes, W. H. (2005). A meta-analysis of the relation of parental involvement to urban elementary school academic achievement. *Urban Education, 40*(3), 237–269.

Kohn, A. (2002). Poor teaching for poor kids. *Language Arts, 79*(3), 251–255.

Mallet, K. E. (2009). *Educational language policy and the role of advocacy among* English Language Professionals *in the United States: An historical and case study analysis.* Unpublished doctoral dissertation, Purdue University, West Lafayette.

Meier, D. (2002). *In schools we trust.* Boston: Beacon Press.

Menken, K. (2008). *English learners left behind: Standardized testing as language policy.* Clevedon, UK: Multilingual Matters.

Reyes, S. A., & Vallone, T. L. (2007). Toward an expanded understanding of two-way bilingual immersion education: Constructing identity through a critical additive bilingual/bicultural pedagogy. *Multicultural Perspectives, 9*(3), 3–11.

Snow, C. (1997). The myths around bilingual education. *NABE News, 21*(2), 29.

Valenzuela, A. (Ed.). (2005). *Leaving children behind: How "Texas-style" accountability fails Latino youth.* New York: State University of New York Press.

10 Not Just One

> **My Dream**
> I dream of the endless universe
> I dream of the splendid earth
> I dream of China
> I dream of my beautiful hometown
> I dream of my smiling relatives
> I dream of my long, long road
> I dream of myself marching on
>
> Written by a fifth-grade Chinese bilingual student

When our bilingual students are empowered to succeed, they are capable of linguistic, academic, and social success. They also have the ability to view life from diverse perspectives—to live not between, but within multiple worlds. This gift is not without cost, as illustrated by the words of the fifth-grade student whose poetry is featured at the beginning of this chapter. Yet in our world filled with ethnic, cultural, and racial strife, what a gift this is!

As our bilingual students grow and change, so do we. Just as their lives will never be the same for living in two worlds, so too will our lives be forever changed by having had the privilege of working with them.

That does not mean these changes come easily. Many years ago, when Sharon first became a bilingual teacher, she quickly realized that her work set her apart from many other educators within her building. As the bilingual kindergarten teacher who taught in the morning, Sharon was responsible for 40 students at one time, without a teaching assistant. Her classroom on the second floor was bare, and she was not given a budget for educational materials. The "mainstream" kindergarten teacher, on the other hand, had 21 students. Her first-floor classroom was well stocked with learning materials suitable for kindergarteners and had a large circle painted on the floor so that the children could easily gather together with their teacher.

Like many bilingual educators, Sharon learned to be resourceful. She was not allowed to paint a circle on the classroom floor, so she created one with masking tape. Her room was soon stocked with learning materials that she collected or purchased on her own. Finally, she found her voice and demanded that the bilingual kindergarten class be divided into two sections of 20 children each. She taught one section in the morning and one in the afternoon. Another teacher was given her former responsibility of teaching an ESL pull-out program in the afternoon.

In her first year, Sharon learned that being a bilingual teacher involves more than teaching; by necessity, it means becoming an advocate for ELLs. That lesson was reinforced many times throughout her career. Years later, when she supported her doctoral studies by traveling to schools and school districts as an educational consultant, she discovered that her experiences as a bilingual teacher were not unique, but were shared by others across her state. In virtually every place that she worked as a consultant, she was approached by at least one bilingual teacher who wanted to talk about the lack of understanding of educational equity for ELLs and how that impacted both bilingual students and bilingual teachers. She was dismayed by the overwhelming sense of marginalization that these educators expressed, but she understood it well.

Although we have seen schools where the needs of ELLs are neither well understood nor addressed, we have also seen schools that could well be national exemplars. In one such school, bilingual students are looked to with admiration, as illustrated in the following vignette:

> The second-grade two-way bilingual immersion classroom had been studying insects through a thematic unit. Today, some of the students were to report, in front of the entire class, on their latest insect observations using the target language—Spanish. As Spanish-dominant Mexican immigrant Marisol stepped forward to do her presentation, sounds of admiration rose from her classmates. Amid the collective "ooos" and "aaahs," one English-dominant child exclaimed, awestruck, "She's soooo good in Spanish!"

In this school, linguistic and cultural diversity are regarded as an asset, not a deficit. Fluent bilingual students are looked to as role models.

This is not always the case. Over the years, Tatyana has also had the opportunity to work with teachers and students in a variety of bilingual settings. Throughout her experiences, she has been struck by students who, unlike Marisol in the previous vignette, have limited awareness of their linguistic talents and bilingual placements, which differentiate them from other students in the school. So when Tatyana had the chance to teach literacy lessons in such schools, she decided to focus on what it meant to be bilingual. She engaged students in this activity a few times at the early elementary level. Often, they did not even realize they were in a bilingual class or understand what that meant. In one particular school, the whole group discussed the meaning of the word *bilingual* in two ways. First, the students were able to understand the meaning of the prefix *bi* through comparison with the word *bicycle*. Second, they compared the English word *bilingual* to the Spanish cognate *bilingüe*. Next, the students individually completed the sentence stem "I am proud to be bilingual because . . ." and came up with a multitude of responses, such as those that follow:

I am proud to be bilingual because I can help my family.

I am proud to be bilingual because I can read more books.

I am proud to be bilingual because I can have lots of friends.

When it was time to share their work, there was a nonstop stream of hands in the air as children eagerly proclaimed pride in their bilingualism.

It is critical to instill this sense of pride in our students early on because of the negative messages they often receive from the dominant culture. Shame of the home language and culture is a feeling that is all too typical among ELLs. Just like bilingual teachers, bilingual students need to be self-aware and proud of what sets them apart.

In the previous pages, we have attempted to address bilingual educators' need for a concise and practical guide to the bilingual classroom. We have presented commonly occurring questions and dilemmas and have responded with suggestions from both researchers and practitioners. In doing so, we have sometimes posed more questions than we have fully answered. It is our hope that you will pursue those answers on your own and that, in the process, you will generate more questions. As you do so, we encourage you to write down your discoveries and share them with us all. We suspect that you will find some of the answers in the words of your students, as in this poem by the graduate of an elementary school Spanish bilingual education program, who went on to continue her language studies at the secondary level at Mandarin:

Not just one

Born into a color
A streak across the vast
Light gray sky
Together, we make a rainbow
Vibrant and youthful

From far away
We may appear the same
Striking colors, unattainable
Like a mirage in the desert
Looking closer, we are a mix
Our hue never changes
Yet as light turns to dark
Variations are created, either bold or fair
We can never be distinguished
We are not just one color

From below no one wants to be us
Trapped forever as just a streak
We are only noticed after a thunderstorm
With furious winds and pounding rain
An up rise of crashing rumbles in the far distance
That no one can understand
But everyone can hear

But, from heaven
Beyond the clouds
Stringing from the rising sun
An intense red glow ends with an infinite blue
There is no precise line
As one color somehow molds and blends into another
Making the entire sky a rainbow
Vibrant and youthful
Striking and strong
Colorful.

By Glenna Adelman Reyes, at age 17

Professional and Support Organizations

American Council on the Teaching of Foreign Languages (ACTFL)
(http://www.actfl.org/)

ACTFL is a national organization dedicated to improving and expanding the instruction of languages in kindergarten through adult education. Its publications include a practitioner journal, *The Language Educator*, which addresses recent trends in the field, and a scholarly research journal, *Foreign Language Annals*. ACTFL's Web site includes information about its annual conventions, along with resources such as a career center, information about professional development sessions, and national and international language learning opportunities for students.

Bilingual/Bicultural Family Network
(http://www.biculturalfamily.org/)

The Bilingual/Bicultural Family Network provides resources, support, and information for families around the world who are raising children in more than one language and culture. It publishes *Multilingual Living Magazine*, a quarterly online journal featuring real-world knowledge, tips, and answers to frequently asked questions, as well as articles by academics and experts in the fields of bilingualism and multilingualism. The primary goal of the Bilingual/Bicultural Family Network is to support families, educators, health providers, and individuals in their efforts to keep heritage languages alive.

Center for Applied Linguistics (CAL)
(http://www.cal.org/)

CAL produces research, tools, and other resources that span the fields of bilingual education, English as a second language, foreign language, and refugee education. Its Web site provides access to databases of national programs, curriculum resources, assessment information, and brochures related to language learning. Publications about diverse cultural groups, programs for language learners, and teaching and learning are also available through the Web site. CAL researchers and educators are involved in many projects and are available to work with schools and districts on technical and professional development.

¡Colorín Colorado!
(http://www.colorincolorado.org/)

¡Colorín Colorado! is a bilingual (Spanish-English) Web site that focuses on biliteracy. It recommends culturally and linguistically relevant literature for Latino students from preschool to the teenage years, as well as informational books specifically for teachers and parents. ¡Colorín Colorado! also summarizes key research related to ELLs and advises families on how to raise their children bilingually and support them in school.

James Crawford's Language Policy Web Site and Emporium
(http://www.languagepolicy.net/)

James Crawford has a long history as an advocate and writer in the field of bilingual education. His personal Web site presents the latest updates on policies and legislation related to ELLs, along with his essays, speeches, and articles on the state of language rights in the United States, and in schools specifically.

Dr. Cummins' ESL and Second Language Learning Web
(http://www.iteachilearn.com/cummins/)

Jim Cummins is a prominent researcher in the field of bilingual education and ESL and an influential theorist of second language acquisition. His Web site posts his latest writing and provides links for related Internet resources.

Institute for Language and Education Policy (ILEP)
(http://www.elladvocates.org/)

ILEP is an organization that advocates research-based policies for English and heritage language learners. Its Web site helps teachers, teacher educators, administrators, parents, and community members to stay informed about current developments in the field. It also provides updates on legislation, research reports, professional presentations, and media coverage related to bilingual education, school reform, language policy, and related issues.

The Internet TESL Journal: For Teachers of English as a Second Language
(http://iteslj.org/)

This electronic teacher-centered journal features teaching strategies, lesson plans, supplemental materials, professional articles, games, educational links for both students and teachers, and comprehensive lists of questions to engage students in a wide range of activities.

Stephen Krashen's Newsletter
(http://sdkrashen.com/)

Stephen Krashen, professor emeritus at the University of Southern California, is an expert in theories of second language acquisition and development. You may sign up for his newsletter to receive the latest commentary on issues related to English and heritage language learners.

National Association for Bilingual Education (NABE)
(http://www.nabe.org/)

NABE, a professional organization of teachers, paraprofessionals, administrators, college students, families, researchers, and advocates, supports bilingual and multicultural education of ELLs through national and state conferences and publications such as the themed magazine *NABE News*. The organization has affiliates at the state and regional level, including CABE (California), NYSABE (New York), and TABE (Texas). Some of these state organizations function as their own entities.

National Association for Multicultural Education (NAME)
(http://www.nameorg.org/)

NAME was established to promote diversity, in all its forms, but especially in education, as a strength of our students, schools, and nation. Its Web site provides links to others that address areas of diversity, such as race, sexuality, gender, and class. In addition to NAME's annual national conference, regional and state chapters also hold meetings and seminars. As a source of research, program overviews, and perspectives in multicultural education, the organization puts out a quarterly journal called *Multicultural Perspectives.*

National Clearinghouse for English Language Acquisition and Language Instruction Educational Programs (NCELA) (http://www.ncela.gwu.edu/)

NCELA is a resource center funded by the U.S. Department of Education that disseminates research, federal grant information, and demographic and statistical data related to ELLs. Information regarding teaching credentials, education policies, and related teaching resources are also available on the Web site. Since passage of the No Child Left Behind Act, NCELA has shifted its focus from bilingual education to English language acquisition.

National Council of Teachers of English (NCTE) (http://www.ncte.org/)

NCTE is devoted to promoting the teaching and learning of English and the language arts. Its Web site has sections specifically devoted to addressing the concerns of elementary, middle, high school, and college educators that address the needs of each student population. It also provides opportunities for advocacy via special events, letter-writing campaigns, and advocacy information. Teachers can also access lesson plans, information on current books, and numerous journals in the field.

PBS Teachers (http://www.pbs.org/teachers/)

Connected to the Public Broadcasting System, this Web site offers teachers a wide range of standards-based resources, detailed lesson plans in various content areas, video clips, and links to related sites. In addition, teachers can join PBS Teacher Connect, an online forum for discussing the integration of digital media and technology in the classroom. The Web site also has links to PBS Kids and PBS Parents.

Teachers of English to Speakers of Other Languages (TESOL) (http://www.tesol.org/s_tesol/index.asp)

TESOL and its affiliates throughout the world are committed to improving ESL and foreign language at all levels. Its Web site provides members with access to ESL standards, lesson plans, and assessments by content area and language skill, as well as employment information. TESOL holds an annual convention that brings together teachers, administrators, and scholars. Its publications include *The Essential Teacher,* a magazine for ESL practitioners and mainstream teachers who work with ELLs, and *TESOL Quarterly,* an academic journal that aims to unite theory and practice in the field. TESOL also has numerous state affiliates.

Mary Ann Zehr's Learning the Language Blog
(http://blogs.edweek.org/edweek/learning-the-language/)

Mary Ann Zehr is an experienced journalist who has written on issues related to language learners for nearly a decade. Her widely read blog can be accessed through *Education Week,* where she is an assistant editor. It highlights recent policy developments related to ELLs and immigrants and includes links to recent articles, books, news briefings, and Web sites and related blogs that she herself follows.

Index

CORWIN

A SAGE Company

The Corwin logo—a raven striding across an open book—represents the union of courage and learning. Corwin is committed to improving education for all learners by publishing books and other professional development resources for those serving the field of PreK–12 education. By providing practical, hands-on materials, Corwin continues to carry out the promise of its motto: **"Helping Educators Do Their Work Better."**